ALDEN HOUSE, DUXBURY.

PILGRIM ALDEN

THE STORY *of* THE LIFE OF THE FIRST JOHN ALDEN IN AMERICA

WITH THE INTERWOVEN STORY OF THE LIFE & DOINGS OF THE PILGRIM COLONY, AND SOME ACCOUNT OF LATER ALDENS

PREPARED UNDER THE DIRECTION OF
AUGUSTUS E. ALDEN

ILLUSTRATED

JAMES H. EARLE & COMPANY
178 WASHINGTON STREET, BOSTON

To the Name of

JOHN ALDEN

And the many Worthy Men who bear It

This Book is dedicated

TABLE of CONTENTS.

PART I.

The PILGRIM CHURCH.

PART II.

PILGRIM ALDEN.

LIST *of* ILLUSTRATIONS.

PREFACE.

There is sometimes a tendency on the part of persons who mistake plebeianism for democracy to deride, as savoring of snobbery, all interest in ancestry and family tradition. It requires little reflection to show the short-sightedness of such an attitude. Among the moral forces which go to make civilized man civilized and not savage, there are few more potent than those which have their source in family ties and traditions. We have only to look back upon Mediaeval Europe to see by how narrow a margin the peoples of those days were saved from degenerate barbarism; and that saving marge lay in the restraints imposed by knightly chivalry and knightly devoir—in an ethic code of caste and station which served to make men noble. And even in our own prosaic day, the day of commonplace comfort, as it has been called, there are instances not a few where the child of an ancient house has been saved from erring by the strength of the hearth-ties, where the failing and the faltering have been reinspired by the resonance of old traditions, where the life of the son's son has been rendered noble by the nobility of the sire. Each of us issues from the complex interweaving of the lives of our fathers and mothers, farther back than reaches the memory of man.

Hidden away in the mind's dim attics are bits of the ancient furnishings and trappings which were the decking of their days. Yet the old furniture is often still substantial, and an ancient mirror, polished anew, is sometimes brought forth, at the unexpected moment, in the unexpected way, revealing us as strangers to ourselves. Perhaps we may never know ourselves, quite as we are, save we polish and brighten the ancient mirrors.

Good old Ebenezer Alden in his "Memorial of the Descendants of the Honorable John Alden," starts out, in the approved mode of the learned treatise, with a definition: "Genealogy is family history; to some a chaos of dry facts; *very dry;* to others, facts revealing principles, laws, methods of the divine government." And then he adds, as if to soften the sour savor of his italics: "Genealogy has its lessons for such as will study them; its uses for such as can appreciate and interpret them." We can agree both with the italics and with the moral. Most genealogies are egregiously dry, but at the same time there are few of them, indeed, which fail to furnish forth material for sermon and for romance—the simple sermon of lives well lived, the thrilling romance of the brave deeds and true loves of those lives. The volume in hand is not a genealogy. It is rather an attempt to give some fragmentary picture of what life meant to two brave hearts that became one for its battles in the very dawn of our national history. Some hint we hope to give, of the races and traditions which produced these two; some sketch of the conditions and chances which threw them together upon the bleak shores of the New World; some touch of their personalities; some tale of their oft-told love, and some count of the children who were born of it.

"I had rather have one drop of Puritan blood in my veins than all that ever flowed in the veins of kings and princes," said John Quincy Adams. And there is not one of all those who like him are sprung from the union of John and Priscilla Alden who would dissent from that saying. For theirs is a precious heritage—the fair name of a brave and honorable sire, the sweet story of a mother's worthy love. Nor need we add that theirs, too, is a precious charge; that it is theirs to see that no dishonor sully so fair a name, that there come no blot upon the family escutcheon.

The principal sources from which the author of this volume has drawn the facts herein set forth, other than such as have been personally communicated by members of the Alden family, are: For the Pilgrim history: Governor Bradford's "History of Plymouth Plantation"; John O. Goodwin's "Pilgrim Republic," and Wm. E. Griffis' "The Pilgrims in Their Three Homes." For matter relating to the Aldens: Justin Winsor's "History of Duxbury"; Rev. Timothy Alden's "A Collection of American Epitaphs and Inscriptions"; Dr. Ebenezer Alden's "Memorial of the descendants of the Hon. John Alden"; Rev. John Alden's "The Story of a Pilgrim Family," and various contributions to the "Mayflower Descendant" and the "New England Historical and Genealogical Register," especially Mrs. Charles L. Alden's "Alden Genealogy" published in the latter periodical.

The author and the book's sponsor also wish to express their thanks to Mr. Edwin S. Crandon, of the staff of the *Boston Transcript*, and to Mrs. Harriet B. Snyder of Tecumseh, Mich., both of Alden lineage, for valuable suggestions and materials; also to Mr. John W. Alden of the Duxbury homestead, for photographic privileges, and to the many other members of the kindred who have by aid and kindly interest furthered the work.

Plymouth Rock, Plymouth.
Pulpit Rock, Clark's Island.

INTRODUCTION.

The three hundred years that have passed since the beginnings of that religious dissent which caused the first peopling of New England have witnessed many changes in human environment and affairs. But not in these alone. We are accustomed to think of what we term human nature as of constant quality and value, always to be counted upon as the same in every estimate of the meaning of human action. When we reflect, however, we see that this is not really the case. Human nature is by no means universally the same and it does change. The nature of the savage is different from that of the civilized man,—for civilization is not merely that veneer which cynical writers so often tell us it is; it is a complex of very real and intimate qualities engrafted upon the essence of the civilized man's personality. Cleanliness is as necessary as food to the comfort of the modern European, but not at all to that of the aborigine. And we often contrast the instinctive industry of the white and yellow races with the no less instinctive idleness of the black and red. Again we contrast Saxon and Celtic temperament — the bull-dog pertinacity of the Englishman with the exuberant good nature of his Irish brother,— for, after all they are brothers; their racial difference is not wider than the Irish Sea. And as between different eras and centuries, each has its characteristic tone and quality which we speak of as the spirit of this age or that — of the Dark Ages, the Renaissance, of the Eighteenth, the Nineteenth centuries. And all of these distinctions refer ultimately to psychological differences in human nature.

Perhaps the most remarkable of all the spiritual revolutions that have ever taken place, and certainly the most noteworthy change in human nature within recent centuries, is the development of humanitarianism, of sympathy of man for man. In the time of Elizabeth mutilation, burning at the stake, disemboweling, were recognized forms of punishment for crime. Torture was still used to exact truthful witness. Pillage and rapine were implied in the definition of war. And the heads of enemies of the state were displayed above London Tower in much the same spirit of vaunting with which the American Indian displayed his scalp trophies. Even two centuries later the insane were treated as criminals, or worse; eleemosynary institutions were comparatively unknown; and there was yet a school of philosophy which taught that animals have neither sense nor feeling, and that no torture brings them pain.

In the Twentieth century, even in civilized lands, there is left brutality enough. But the conscience of the world has been awakened, and men have come to sympathize with one another and to feel responsibility for the sufferings of their fellows. Perhaps this is because the human organism is become more delicately responsive to influences from without, so that whether they will or no men are forced to share the pains of each other. But in any case a new spirit of tolerance and compassion has developed which is the fairest promise for the future worth of the human race.

Charity and tolerance grow step by step with sympathy. In 1600 there was but one land in the civilized world where religious liberty could be found. And in the Dutch Republic it existed less from principle than from practical need, for the Holland of that day was sore pressed by her Spanish overlord, and was ready at any price to secure the hands which would help her industries or arms to throw off the Spanish yoke.

It was to Holland that the intolerance of England first drove that little band of religious outcasts which we know as the Pilgrim Fathers. Poverty and the desire for a purer atmosphere and a freedom to grow, in turn urged them on to America.

In searching out the beginnings of that slow-spreading evolution of the spirit of compassion which has been and is gradually kneading the whole world into one human folk, there is to be found no more significant story than that of the Pilgrim Church. The Fathers were not men of our country, nor of our type or nature; and we must not judge them as such. Austere they were, almost to asceticism. Fanatic we might call them today, and bigoted. But in the age in which they lived they were first in liberal charity, and their early history abounds in instances of devotion and service, not only to one another, but to strangers and yet those who used them ill, which are not exceeded in nobility by the finest examples in human annals. Certain defences were necessary to the preservation of the foundling colony, but in so far as they could they established a city of refuge for all who were oppressed and a church of toleration in the wilderness. And when, in an age yet to come, clannish patriotism and pride of race shall have given way to a broader pride in a nobler humanhood — when in place of Saxon, Mongol, or

Slav, man's ideal shall be Man,—the Rock of Landing will be honored not merely as the threshold of a great civic state, but as a stepping-stone in the progress of humankind toward its final Republic, to be founded in mutual tolerance, sympathy and love.

CHAPTER I.

THE CHURCH IN ENGLAND.

ECCLESIASTICAL England in the reign of Elizabeth was divided into warring factions. Tables were turned against the Catholics who had been dominant in Mary's time, and they were well nigh driven to cover. But the Protestant Church of England was already become as a house divided against itself, and when James I ascended the throne he found two clearly defined parties within the authorized fold. These parties were the Conformists, or High Ritualists, and the Noncomformists, or Puritans. The Conformists wished to develop the church as nearly as possible on the model of the Church of Rome, and to this end insisted upon the sanctity and significance of the church ceremonies and exalted the authority of the church itself and of the King as its earthly head.

The Puritans, on the other hand, objected to showy ceremonies, especially such as seemed still to imply allegiance to rejected tenets of the Romish Church. The King naturally favored that party which was inclined to magnify his position and powers, and in consequence the Puritan clergy were hard pressed, many of them being ruined by the despotic regulations enforced upon them and nearly all being driven from their holdings. But this despotism aroused the laity. Puritanism became a political as well as a religious movement, and during the entire reign of James I the political Puritans were a majority in the House of Commons. The controlling hand they did not get, however, until the time of Cromwell, when long years of tyranny and injustice had brought on not only political reaction and revolution, but to the hurt of the race, that spirit of morose and gloomy piety for which the name "Puritan" has ever since stood,— a spirit which was to render "Merrie England" in the old Elizabethan sense forevermore impossible, and to strangle in its first vigor that genius for song which might have made England instead of Germany the mother of the music of the civilized world, now, as she was then. It was the price of English liberty, however, for it was the Puritans alone in those unquiet days who warded the sacred fire.

That is, in England. In America the nurture of liberty was first entrusted to other hands. In the realm of King James there were, beside Conformists and Puritans, certain religious reformers variously known as Separatists, Independents, and Brownists,— the latter name being applied to the followers of an Independent preacher named Brown, and from these extended to include other Independent congregations. The Separatists did not differ in the fundamentals of their faith from either party adhering to the Church of England, but they did differ in their conception of church government, and above all they objected to the notion that there could be an earthly head to any spiritual organization. As a consequence of this iconoclasm, the Separatists incurred the displeasure both of Puritan and Conformist, and they were hanged and banished with such a hearty good will that the sect — never large — soon disappeared altogether. At the accession of James I there remained in the whole of Britain but one of their congregations — the church at Gainsborough, a town some fifty miles from London; and two years later, in 1605, even this church was forced to flee to Holland for safety. But a fragment of the congregation remained behind, at the hamlet of Scroo-

SCROOBY.

by, a few miles west of Gainsborough, and out of this fragment was to grow the final and most fateful fruition of the Separatist movement — the Church of the Pilgrim Fathers.

The hamlet of Scrooby was a post-station on the Great Northern Road which led from London to the "North Country." It was the business of the "post," as the post-officer was then called, to tend the forwarding of the court mails, and to entertain travelers and supply them with horses at a rental of three pence per mile — a traffic which was reserved as a government monopoly. From 1590 to 1607 the "post" at Scrooby was William Brewster, the son of William Brewster, who had held the office before him. In his younger days Brewster, Jr., had been attached to the service of Secretary of State Davison, and with him had been in Holland on diplomatic business.

But when Davison had fallen under the displeasure of Elizabeth, Brewster retired to the seclusion of Scrooby and there, in due time, succeeded to his father's position.

Brewster was then a Puritan, and he interested himself in building up the churches in the vicinity, many of which were without pastors and were fallen into decay. The church of his own choice and attendance was that presided over by Richard Clifton at Babworth, some four miles walk through the fields. Here he was accustomed to take his young friend, William Bradford, an orphaned son of a well-to-do yeoman of the Yorkshire village of Austerfield, two and a half miles north of Scrooby. Bradford had come to Brewster when a mere boy, in search of a spiritual companionship and sympathy which his native village did not afford. And without doubt the scholarly attainments and exquisite style of the future governor of Plymouth and author of its earliest history were largely the consequence of this early contact with a man who had been educated at Cambridge and who had been attached to the gay court of Elizabeth. And we can as little question that Brewster, on his part, was but too well pleased with a pupil of Bradford's aptitude and promise.

In 1606 the Puritans, even in such country places as Scrooby, were made to feel the heavy hand of the prelatical authorities. Many of the clergy were driven from their charges, and among them Richard Clifton. There were still around Scrooby a few members of the Separatist congregation which had fled from Gainsborough. With these Brewster and his friends joined and with Clifton as pastor, a Separatist Church was formed. As junior pastor, one John Robinson, a Master of Arts and Bachelor of Divinity from Corpus Christi College, Cambridge, was shortly after secured, and he is credited with having been " the most learned, polished and modest spirit " ever connected with the Independent movement.

At first, meetings were held in the ancient Episcopal manor house which was then transformed into the post-station. But the congregation was not to be left at peace. Informants were not wanting, and by the autumn of 1607 this church, like its predecessor, had found its one hope for survival lay in flight to Holland. But even that flight must be secret, for the King, to prevent such emigrations, had closed all ports against whoever had no license to depart.

A ship was hired to take on the fugitives at Boston, forty miles from Scrooby. But the captain proved them false, bargained with the officers, and delivered the people over to the authorities by whom they were robbed of well nigh all they had and turned away, with exception of seven of the leaders, after a month's imprisonment.

A second attempt at flight, in the spring of 1608, was even less happy. A Dutch captain was bribed to embark the congregation at Grimsby Common, a tract of vacant land near the mouth of the river Humber. A single boat-load, among whom was Bradford, had been taken aboard when an armed posse appeared in pursuit of the fugitives. The captain of the vessel, in fear, and despite the pleadings of those on board, hoisted his sails and fled. A storm arose and carried the ship so far out of her course as the shores of Norway, but eventually she reached Holland. But the main part of the congregation was still in England. At the approach of the posse the men had fled, as only thus could they be saved from imprisonment and their little property from ruinous fines. The women and children, after enduring the process of what then passed for justice, were allowed to go free.

It was seen that the church could not emigrate in a body, and other tactics were resorted to. Singly and by families they were smuggled out of England, Clifton, Brewster and Robinson being the last to go, and finally, in August, the self-expatriated band were reunited in Amsterdam. Here was completed the first stadium of their Pilgrimage, and here began the second epoch in their history.

CHAPTER II.

PILGRIMS IN HOLLAND.

N 1608 the Dutch Republic was just entering upon its twelve years truce in the long war with Spain, and its cities, prosperous even in war time, were rapidly growing in wealth and commercial importance. At that period the industrial skill, learning and civilization of Western Europe were largely centered in the Low Countries, and especially in manufactures did the Hollanders excel. But years of war had weakened the industrial forces of the country, and on this account, as well as because Spanish intolerance had taught the Dutch people the value of religious liberty, refugees from England were welcome immigrants in their cities.

When the Scrooby congregation reached Amsterdam — to them, raw countrymen as most of them were, a veritable city of marvels — they found two Separatist churches already established there. One of these, presided over by Pastor Johnson, assisted by Henry Ainsworth, the foremost Hebrew scholar of the time, had been banished from London in 1593. The other was the congregation which had emigrated from Gainsborough.

At first the new-comers purposed settling in Amsterdam. But it shortly developed that their brethren were not wholly at peace with one another, nor altogether in sympathy with them. The larger church was split into factions, the quarrel centering about the apparel of Pastor Johnson's wife. The more zealous members were sore mortified that she should affect such vanities as stays and starch, and a velvet hood was esteemed a veritable gage of the devil. At the same time the pastor of the church from Gainsborough, the Rev. John Smith, was bitterly opposed to the spirit of toleration which animated Robinson and his people. The latter, therefore, deemed it best to remove from the scene of discord; and in May of 1609, permission to immigrate having been obtained from the city of Leyden, they removed thither. But in Amsterdam they left Clifton, worn out at the age of fifty-six; and doubtless some few of the congregation remained with him.

Leyden was at that time the second city in importance in free Holland. Its manufactures were largely of textile fabrics, especially linen and woolen goods, but it was also a great centre for the printing of books, and its university, gift of the Prince of Orange, was already drawing students from foreign lands. While unskilled labor was here less in demand than in the great seaport which they had left, still there was little difficulty in securing employment, and the members of the Pilgrim band were soon comfortably established in their new abode. For the most part they set about acquiring handicrafts.

Bradford apprenticed himself to a baize-maker, eventually carrying on the manufacture of baize in his own right. Elder Brewster's son, Jonathan, became a ribbon weaver; John Tilly worked in silk, and William White, Robert Cushman and others, in wool; Degory Priest was a hatter; John Jenny a brewer; and William Jepson and Francis Eaton took up carpentering. It is hard at this late day to say what this education in practical industries must have meant to the New World colonists later on, but it is certain that no better training could have been devised for them. They were already farmers, and now they were acquiring first-hand knowledge of the most advanced industrial methods of their day. And even if there was to be no immediate call for the exercise of the handicrafts they were acquiring, in the wilderness which they were to settle, still the broadening influence of their training could not but have increased their resourcefulness and adaptability many fold.

William Brewster early came in contact with the University of Leyden, where he found employment teaching English to Dutch and Danish students. In connection with this work he wrote one of the first grammars of the English language, modeled after the Latin grammar of the period. And both he and John Robinson, the pastor, soon matriculated in the University as students, the one of literature and the other of theology. This afterwards proved of no small advantage to Brewster, for University membership carried with it a number of privileges,— among others freedom in publication and immunity from arrest except by the officers of the University — privileges which served him well when later King James sought to lay hold on him.

In their new home the Pilgrims prospered to such an extent that in two years (May, 1611) four of their number — John Robinson, William Jepson, Henry Wood, and Randolph Tickens — were able to purchase house and land almost under the walls of Leyden University. It is probable that these four were merely agents for the whole community, for houses were erected upon the vacant land, the original being the pastor's home and meeting-house,—to accommodate them all. At the present day the site is occupied by a French Protestant church, but a marble slab still commemorates Pastor Robinson, who died there in 1625.

In 1616 Brewster set up a printing establishment, possibly in partnership with one Thomas Brewer. During the three years of its existence about fifteen books and pamphlets were issued from this press. Most of these were for the propagation of religious ideas, in England esteemed nothing short of incendiary. Especially was this true of certain pamphlets criticising King James's religious polity. As the books attained a wide circulation in London and elsewhere in England, it was not long before determined effort was made by the English authorities to stem the tide of insubordinate literature at its source.

At first Brewster's University membership saved him from the clutches of the English ambassador, but the Dutch were anxious to strengthen their alliance with King James, and when the English insisted, permitted the seizure and confiscation of

Brewster's printing effects. Fortunately Brewster himself was in London at the time, the summer of 1619, and so escaped. But his printing was at an end.

It was while Brewster was still in the printing business, in 1617, that he took into his office Edward Winslow, a young Englishman of education, who, visiting Leyden, had cast in his lot with Robinson's congregation. Perhaps the charms of Elizabeth Barker had most to do with this move, for the next year she was married to Winslow.

Another addition to the company during their sojourn in Leyden, and one who was to be of no small value to them in the New World, was Captain Myles Standish. Captain Standish had been commissioned in his youth by Queen Elizabeth to serve with the English troops which she sent to the aid of Holland. He had probably lived there from that time on. Of a keen, fiery disposition, restive under any restraint save the military, but a soldier to the crest of his morion, it is difficult to see just what it was in the Pilgrim community which drew him to them.

More than likely the ill-starred Rose, his first wife, was of the company, and he, as Winslow, was conquered by Cupid, even more puissant than

Mars. Mrs. Stowe, in her delicious Phineas Fletcher, has given us a rough modern counterpart of the good captain's first romance.

Intermarriage brought others beside Winslow and Standish into the community. Not only did the young men take them wives from among their English co-religionists in Amsterdam, but not a few of them found the buxom maids of Holland and the dark-eyed daughters of French Huguenots — refugees like themselves — fair in their eyes. Altogether there are no fewer than fifty marriages recorded for the company during their twelve years stay in Holland — a promising record for a church numbering not more than three hundred communicants in its best period.

But the marryings in were counterweighed by marryings out. And the more adventurous of the young men were enlisting in the Dutch army or seeking service in her merchant marine. The children, too, were growing up with Dutch notions of morality,— and Continental moral ideals have ever been more lax than English. In these symptoms the graver heads of the community saw signs of the gradual absorption of their people into the Dutch nationality. Now they had never ceased to be English in sentiment and sympathy, and their dearest wish was to be able to live under the banner of St. George.

When we add to these considerations the fact that with all their industry and sobriety there was no prospect for any permanent improvement in their condition, that in Holland they who in England had largely been free farmers were condemned to remain hand-workers and wage-earners — the class first like to suffer in the war that was about to break out afresh between Holland and Spain; in view of all this, it is no wonder that they shortly set about planning a new Pilgrimage.

This time their eyes were turned toward the New World. In 1618 an attempt was made through the Virginia Company to secure from King James a charter permitting them to settle in its territory. Nothing came of it. A second attempt was frustrated by prelatical objection to the Congregational mode of church government. But James was not at all averse to having his trans-Atlantic domain developed by a colony that so fairly promised self-support and prosperity, especially in view of previous expensive failures, and when the seven articles acknowledging his sovereignty and authority and subscribing to the creed of the Church of England had been received from the church in Ley-

DELFTHAVEN

den, a patent was at length issued permitting them to settle in the northernmost part of Virginia, then extending to Long Island Sound.

There were yet delays. But finally one Thomas Weston of London formed a company of merchants who were to furnish the money for the expedition, and at the end of seven years receive one-half of all the properties acquired by the settlers. These men, who entered into the project as a speculation, were styled "the adventurers," and articles of agreement between them and the Pilgrims were drawn up and signed.

Not all of the Leyden church were to go. Only some four score of the more youthful and vigorous were to embark. The majority of the congregation, with Pastor Robinson, remained in Holland, — some to follow in later expeditions, some to end their days there. But when, on or near the last day of July, 1620, the colonists loaded their goods upon canal boats and proceeded along the waterways of green Holland to Delftshaven, where the sixty-ton pinnace "Speedwell" waited to take them to England, Robinson and his whole congregation accompanied them.

At Delftshaven passed the day and the night of the parting. There was religious service and counselings; there was a farewell banquet given to those departing by their brethren who were to remain; there were tears and sorrow as well, for many a parting was to be the last. And so, wrote Governor Bradford, who was of the departing band, "they left that goodly and pleasant city which had been their resting-place near twelve years; but they knew that they were Pilgrims, and looked not much on those things, but lifted up their eyes to the heavens, their dearest country, and quieted their spirits."

MODEL OF THE MAYFLOWER, PILGRIM HALL.

CHAPTER III.

THE VOYAGE OF THE MAYFLOWER

THE Speedwell, according to the design of the Adventurers, was to remain with the new colony; and her crew, under Captain Reynolds, had been hired for one year. First she was to proceed to Southampton and there, joining the Mayflower, start on the long voyage across the ocean. This stage of the journey was accomplished without incident, and the wanderers were soon in the presence of the vessel which their Pilgrimage was to make famous.

The Mayflower was rated at a hundred and eighty tons,— about one hundred and twenty tons, modern rating. Yet for those days she was accounted a fine ship. In all England there were not then many vessels of two hundred tons, and the Mayflower was larger than most ships crossing the Atlantic. Her master was Captain Jones, a seafaring gentleman of piratical antecedents, but familiar with American coasts and waters.

At Southampton the Pilgrims were joined by a small company who had cast their lot with the new venture, among them young John Alden, who was to play such a large role in the future of the colony. These, with some of the brethren who had been in England, were already on the Mayflower,—just laden for her departure. Ninety of the new-comers were taken on the larger vessel, with John Carver as their governor, while thirty, William Martin being governor, remained on the Speedwell.

But the time of setting forth was yet delayed. There were modifications in the Articles of Agreement which Weston, who had engineered the enterprise, wished to force upon the colonists to their disadvantage and the company's greater profit. When he found that the Pilgrims would not submit to petty tyranny, he left them in a rage to "stand upon their own legs." This forced them to pay port charges, and it was only by selling most of their supply of butter that they were able to clear the port, and even then they were left with inadequate outfittings.

But on August fifteen, 1620, the two vessels put to sea. Four days out, Captain Reynolds of the Speedwell reported his ship as leaking dangerously. Accordingly they bore up for Dartmouth and spent ten days at that port discharging, repairing and restowing the Speedwell, although no serious damage was discovered. The voyage was resumed, but three hundred miles beyond Land's End Reynolds again reported a leak, and forced the company to put back to Plymouth. There the vessel was again overhauled, but no special leak found.

Reynolds and his crew, however, refused to take her to the New World, and as the season was advancing it was determined to send her back to London and to proceed on the voyage without her. Eighteen of her passengers went back with her, but twelve were crowded into the Mayflower; and for the third time the good ship headed westward.

This was on September sixteen. The passengers were all in good health, excepting for temporary seasickness, and there is a story handed down that one of the crew who used to rail at and curse them while in this condition, expressing the hope that he might have the privilege of throwing their bodies into the sea, died very shortly after the voyage was begun. In their comrade's fate his fellows took warning.

At first fair weather favored the voyagers, but about midway of the Atlantic the Mayflower encountered a succession of severe storms. During one of these storms a beam amidship was sprung. The sailors, in alarm, were for turning back to England. But it was as far to Europe as to America. At this juncture a carpenter of the colonists came to the rescue. He had brought from Holland a jack-screw, an implement hardly known among the English of the time, and with the aid of this the damage was repaired and the ship continued on her course.

But the voyage was not without its haps and mishaps. The continuous stormy weather kept the passengers cooped below decks most of the time, and on one occasion John Howland, finding the confinement irksome, ventured above. In the roll of the ship he was thrown overboard. Fortunately the coil of the topsail halyard was trailing in the sea. Howland caught this and was finally drawn aboard. There was one death among the Pilgrims during the voyage. This was of William Button, servant or apprentice to Dr. Fuller, the company's physician. Button died November sixteen, but Oceanus Hopkins, son to Stephen and Elizabeth Hopkins, was born at sea,—and so the tale of the colonists remained the same.

On the morning of November twenty, land was sighted. Beautifully wooded hills were seen sloping down to the waters of the sea — a welcome vision after more than two months of ocean monotone. Captain Jones recognized the land as Cape Cod, which was already well known to mariners and had been charted by Captain John Smith and others.

Finding that the Mayflower was far north of her destination, her course was changed, and for half a day she headed southward. The only result was a baffled search for a passage through the shoals and currents off the elbow of the Cape, and Captain Jones professed himself unable to find a safe course to the mouth of the Hudson.

A consultation was held among the leaders. Winter was drawing on and many of the company began already to show signs of the disease which was soon to cut in half their number. It was decided that a landing must be effected as early as possible, even if they were forced to abandon their project of settling within the territory of the Virginia Company. Accordingly the Mayflower put about and headed for Cape Cod Harbor, where now is Provincetown.

It was held as early as 1669 that Jones had been hired by the Dutch to break his agreement and carry the colonists far north of the Dutch province of Manhattan. In that year Nathaniel Morton, secretary of Plymouth Colony, professes to have "late and certain intelligence" to this effect. But neither Bradford nor Winslow make mention of any such fraud or suspicion of it, and it is now generally believed that stormy weather had more to do with the settling of New England than providential Dutchmen.

Their change of destination created a new problem for the Pilgrims. Settlements in that day were all under some form of patent, grant or charter, and these furnished their legal basis and fixed their status with reference to the home government. In landing north of the forty-first parallel the colonists were placing themselves beyond the scope and protection of the King's patent. Although James, in a general way, asserted sovereignty over it, New England was then practically no man's land, and settlers landing there without patent or grant could form nothing but a foundling colony.

But the Pilgrims were equal to the emergency. The men gathered together in the cabin of the Mayflower and drew up and signed the famous Compact which was to serve as the legal basis of their emprise. This Compact, which John Quincy Adams described as "perhaps the only instance in human history of that positive, original social com-

SIGNING COMPACT IN CABIN OF THE MAYFLOWER.

pact which speculative philosophers have imagined as the only legitimate source of government," ran as follows:

In ye name of God, Amen! We whose names are under-writen, the loyall subjects of our dread soveraigne Lord, King James, by ye grace of God, of Great Britaine, Franc, & Ireland king, defender of ye faith, etc., having undertaken, for ye glorie of God and advancement of ye Christian faith, and honour of our king and countrie, a voyage to plant ye first colonie in ye Northerne parts of Virginia, doe by these presents solemnly and mutualy in ye presence of God, and one of another, covenant and combine ourselves togeather into a civill body politick, for our better ordering and preservation and furtherance of ye ends aforesaid; and by virtue hereof to enacte, constitute, and frame such just and equall lawes, ordinances, acts, constitutions, and offices, from time to time, as shall be thought most meete and convenient for ye generall good of ye Colonie, unto which we promise all due submission and obedience.

In witness wherof we have hereunder subscribed our names at Cap-Codd ye I.I. of November, in ye year of ye raigne of our soveraigne lord, King James, of England, France, & Ireland ye eighteenth, and of Scotland ye fiftie-fourth. An. Dom. 1620.

The signers of this compact were: John Carver, William Bradford, Edward Winslow, William Brewster, Isaac Allerton, Myles Standish, John Alden, Samuel Fuller, Christopher Martin, William Mullins, William White, Richard Warren, John Howland, Stephen Hopkins, Edward Tilley, John Tilley, Francis Cook, Thomas Rogers, Thomas Tinker, John Rigdale, Edward Fuller, John Turner, Francis Eaton, James Chilton, John Crackston, John Billington, Moses Fletcher, John Goodman, Degory Priest, Thomas Williams, Gilbert Winslow, Edmund Margeson, Peter Brown, Richard Britteridge, George Soule, Richard Clarke, Richard Gardiner, John Allerton, Thomas English, Edward Dotey, Edward Lister.

While the foundations of the new colony—aye, of a new nation! — were thus being laid, the vessel had rounded the point of the Cape and come to anchor within a mile of the site of Provincetown.

. This was on the twenty-first of November, 1620. More than a hundred days had elapsed since the departure from Delftshaven; ninety-nine from Southampton; and sixty-seven since Plymouth had faded from their view. The voyage of the Mayflower was at an end, and the New World was before them.

CHAPTER IV.

PILGRIMS IN AMERICA.

T WAS fortunate that the winter of 1620-1621 was exceptionally mild. Had it been severe it is not likely that the Pilgrim colony would have survived it; for the long sea voyage, the bad air of cabin life, and a surfeit of salt food, had so undermined the health of most of the company that there was left little strength to withstand the rigors of harsh winter weather. Even as it was the deaths were all too many.

The condition of their people made the Pilgrim leaders anxious to land as soon as possible, and they immediately set about preparing expeditions to explore the coast for a suitable location for their settlement. While a sloop which had been brought, in pieces, between decks, was being set up, a land exploration under Captain Standish was undertaken. The company consisted of twenty men, each armed with sword and musket, and it started on its venture November twenty-five, 1620. After journeying a mile along the shore the men saw the first Indians encountered — a band of five or six, who fled at their approach.

The first day of their journey was without other event. On the twenty-sixth their earliest discovery of importance was of a number of springs of fresh water in the valley where, in after time, stood the village of East Harbor. They had been without drink since leaving the Mayflower and suffered much from thirst. Later in the day they discovered sassafras — a plant at that time much valued in Europe for medicinal purposes — and signs of both Indian and European habitation. The latter consisted of the remains of a house, and a great ship's kettle, indicating that the inhabitants had been sailors. It was near this ruin that they found cached several bushels of maize. It was the first they had seen, and the finding was really providential, for it was from this corn that the first Plymouth crop was planted. The explorers with a little hesitation, took possession of the find, stowing it in the great kettle for transportation. Later on the Indian owner was paid double value for his loss. They continued their journey as far as the Pamet River, where they found further token of European occupation in the shape of a rude fortification. Burdened as they were, it was useless to continue the advance, so at this point they turned back toward the vessel. After a night of rainy encampment the party concealed the burdensome kettle of corn, put in order the muskets dampened by the rain, and marched shipward. They reached the Mayflower's landing-place early in the evening.

It was yet ten days before the shallop was ready for coast-wise exploration. When on Monday, December seven, it at length put off, Captain Jones in his long boat accompanied, and was made leader of the expedition. Almost at once stormy weather was encountered, and the party put into East Harbor for the night. In a freezing snow storm they marched overland several miles in search of shelter and a number caught the beginnings of their death-illness from this exposure.

The next day they proceeded to the mouth of the Pamet River. The land which it drained was explored to within a mile of the Atlantic, and several of the party were in favor of settling on this stream. The brackishness of the water, however, and the shallowness of the harbor, were considerations of sufficient weight to cause the majority to vote for a continuance of the explorations. The corn, concealed by the first expedition, together with an added supply which was discovered, was sent to the Mayflower in charge of Captain Jones, returning.

The body of the expedition spent some further time in searching out the country, and again found traces both of white and Indian occupation, the former being this time the remains of a sailor buried with aboriginal honors. But although the Pilgrims were anxious to establish communication with the natives, none of these were to be found, and on December tenth the expedition returned to the Mayflower. During their absence had been born Peregrine White, the first native Yankee, who was to live to the good old age of four score and four. Doubtless he was a much-coddled youngster.

Before the third exploration was under way death had begun its dark ministration. On the fourteenth Edward Thompson, who was in service to the father of baby Peregrine, passed away, and on the sixteenth, when the explorers started forth, Jasper More was dying. Ere the party should return, Dorothy Bradford, whose husband was of the explorers, was to have sunk beneath the waves, and James Chilton to have closed his eyes forever. And these were only the first of the winter's victims.

The members of the second expedition had sighted the hill Manomet on the south side of Plymouth Harbor. One Coppin, a sailor, who had been upon the coast before, vaguely remembered a harbor which he thought might lie beyond this hill. Accordingly Manomet was made the objective point of the new exploration.

With the cold was again their first toil; for two of the eighteen men were overcome by it while the party was battling with head-winds and acquiring the armor of ice with which the freezing spray encoated them; they were able, with some difficulty, to effect a landing and encamp for the night. Several Indians were seen busied with a stranded grampus, but these ran away when the shallop approached.

A strict watch was kept during the night, although the company was not disturbed. The next day the men divided, ten by land and eight by boat exploring Wellfleet Bay. At night the two parties again came together and encamped once more on Eastham beach. It was in the early dawn that they were roused by one of their comrades with the cry of "Indians! Indians!" The war-cry of the savages even then mingled with the sentinel's alarm.

Most of the men had left their muskets in the shallop, and now ran for them fighting off the savages with their swords; but Standish and three others had their guns by them and opened fire. A sharp skirmish ensued before the Indians were driven off, but none of the explorers were hurt. The place of the encampment was thenceforth called "The First Encounter."

Putting to sea once more the party fell in with rough water and snow. The rudder hinges were broken and the steering had to be done by oar. The mast broke, too, and carried the sail overboard. Still they held on their course and late in the day made the entrance of Plymouth Harbor (this name had already been given it by Captain John Smith). Here Coppin, the pilot, was dismayed to find the place altogether strange to him, and the boat was very near destruction.

The cool head of one of the steersmen, however, saved them, and a landing was effected on Clark's Island, so called after the sailor who was first to set foot on shore. The next day was Saturday, and the company rested on the island. On Monday, December twenty-one, the first landing was made on Plymouth Rock and the site of the future settlement explored. The prime requirement of the settlers was a good harbor, and this they had seen that Plymouth afforded.

But they also desired plenty of fresh water, fertile fields, and an easily defensible position. A survey of the land showed all of these. There were broad cornfields, already cleared for cultivation, which had been abandoned by the Patuxet Indians some three years before. Through the fields a number of brooks and runlets coursed to the sea, affording a bountiful supply of the purest water.

Finally a steep hill, over one hundred and fifty feet high, furnished an ideal site for a fort which should command the entire reach of open country round about. Well satisfied with the result of their search, the explorers passed one more night in camp and then hastened back to the waiting Mayflower.

On December twenty-six, after an unsuccessful attempt the day before, the Mayflower reached her final destination and dropped anchor in Plymouth Harbor. The next day was Sunday and there was no disembarking. The two or three days following were devoted to the determining of the exact site of the future village, there being some difference of opinion among the voters, and it was not until January second that its actual laying out and building was begun.

In 1627 De Rasieres, of the Dutch colony of Manhattan, visited and described Plymouth. " New Plymouth," he wrote, " lies on the slope of a hill, stretching east toward the sea-coast, with a broad street about a cannon-shot of eight hundred feet long leading down the hill, with a crossing in the middle, northward to the rivulet and southward to the land.

" The houses are constructed of hewn planks, with gardens also enclosed behind and at the sides with hewn planks, so that their houses and courtyards are arranged in very good order, with a stockade against a sudden attack; and at the ends of the streets there are three wooden gates. In the centre, on the cross street, stands the Governor's house, before which is a square enclosure upon which four pateros are mounted, so as to flank along the streets.

"Upon the hill they have a large square house with a flat roof, made of thick sawn planks stayed with oak beams, upon the top of which they have six cannons, which shoot iron balls of four and five pounds and command the surrounding country. The lower part they use for their church, where they preach on Sundays and the usual holidays." The main street, now Leyden Street, was at first called simply "The Street." The first building to be erected upon it was a large common house, twenty feet square, in which, on January thirty-one, 1621, was held the first religious worship on shore, of the whole Pilgrim band. They had no minister with them, but Elder Brewster preached, then, as he continued to do for several years to come. The palisade and fort which De Rasieres mentions were, of course, not constructed this first winter, but Fort Hill (now Burial Hill) was fortified and the cannon mounted there.

The building of the settlement was not uninterrupted nor uneventful. On the contrary it was carried on under the severest trials. From December to April the death rate averaged four a week. By January first there had been six deaths. During that month there were eight more. In February there were seventeen; in March thirteen; and during the rest of the year six. One-half of all the passengers of the Mayflower died this first year. Nor was the disease, in nearly every case pulmonary consumption, confined to the passengers, for a large part of the men under Jones were ill also, and many of them died.

In the colony at one time there were only seven well persons, among them Standish and Brewster, to tend their fellows. It is no wonder if the first house erected, converted into a hospital, but feebly answered the need. Among the last to die was the Colony's first governor, John Carver. This was in April after the planting was begun. William Bradford was elected to succeed him, and was destined to fill the office every year thereafter, save three only, until his death in 1657. Before the summer of 1621 was over Mrs. Carver was laid beside her husband. It is worthy of note that of the eighteen wives and mothers in the Pilgrim band, fourteen were among the first winter's dead.

Friendly relations with the Indians were early established. Stray savages had been seen from time to time, but it was not until March twenty-six that communication was actually opened with them. On that day an Indian walked boldly into the settlement and greeted the colonists with the English word "Welcome!" The visitor was a Maine Indian named Samoset who had learned his little English from fishermen on the Maine coast. He was at the time on a visit to the Cape Indians.

Through Samoset intercourse was established

with the Sachem Massasoit, chief of the confederated tribes of Pokanoket — the Indian name for all the territory from Narraganset Bay to the end of Cape Cod. Indeed, on April first, Massasoit himself visited the colony and was induced to enter into an alliance with the Pilgrims and to take an oath of allegiance to King James.

To these pledges the sachem ever remained faithful, and it is hardly to be doubted that Plymouth owed her early prosperity, if not her very existence, to this chieftain's friendship. The friendship of the Indians aided the colonists in yet another way, for it added to their community two very useful citizens, Squantum, or Tisquantum, and Hobomok. The first of these had been to England on a trading vessel and he spoke English very well. It was he who instructed the white men how to cultivate maize. Hobomok was early attached to the household of Myles Standish, and taught the redoubtable captain the Indian language. Both of these savages ended their days with the whites.

The summer of 1621 passed peacefully and prosperously. There was an exploring expedition which went as far as Boston Harbor; there were trading trips to the native villages, and on one occasion Edward Winslow and Stephen Hopkins made a diplomatic visit to Massasoit. But for the most part the Pilgrims stayed at home and tended their crops, which flourished accordingly.

After the harvest, was held the first New England Thanksgiving. Huntsmen brought in a supply of game; the Indian allies of the colonists were invited, and for three days the company made merry with sports and feasting. Late in November of this year came the ship Fortune bringing thirty-five new colonists, for the most part young men. As these had brought no subsistence with them, their support was foisted upon the Colony. Owing to the excellence of their crops, this would have proved no great burden to the settlers, had promised supplies reached them. But the supplies were not sent, and before the next summer came the colonists were reduced by their generosity to but scanty fare.

Early in 1622 came rumors of trouble with the Narragansett Indians. Their sachem, Canonicus, sent his famous war gage, a sheaf of arrows bound about with a rattle-snake skin, to Governor Bradford, and received the Governor's significant reply — the skin filled with powder and shot. This overawed the Indians for the time, but the settlers did not feel safe from attack until they had erected the palisade which De Rasieres described in 1627. This work was completed in February.

When spring came, sixty acres of corn were planted. But the colony was already suffering for food, and Winslow and others made a number of trips for the purpose of buying corn from the natives, with some success. To add to Plymouth's burden, however, the summer brought sixty men who were to establish a second colony under Weston's management, and these were left in Plymouth until a site for their settlement should be selected. As they robbed the Plymouth fields for roasting ears, and made no manner of restitution, the corn crop was badly damaged, and when harvested was found inadequate to the winter's need.

The year 1623 was a noteable one in the history of the Colony. It began with semi-famie and renewed Indian troubles. The men sent out by Weston the summer before had established themselves at Weymouth, and there by abuse and unfair dealing, had speedily aroused the hostility of the native tribes.

Further they soon wasted the plentiful supply of food with which they had been furnished by the promoters of their colony, and the hostile savages were not slow to see their advantage in the ensuing weakness and want. A league was formed and the destruction of the whites of both colonies plotted.

Adding to Plymouth's danger, her friend Massasoit, was sick, as it was thought, unto death. It was at this time that the reported presence of a Dutch ship on the south coast induced Winslow to journey thither. He did not find the Dutchman, but he was enabled to visit and cure Massasoit. In return the whites were told all the particulars of the conspiracy, which the sachem, in his enfeebled condition, had been unable to thwart. The result of this information was Myles Standish's famous expedition to Weymouth and the slaying of Wituwamet and his fellow conspirators. This ended the Indian troubles until King Phillip's War many years later.

The question of food was still paramount. The shortage of grain was even worse than the year before, and when summer came the main reliance of the colonists was on clams and other shell fish. In order to insure a more adequate supply of corn for the ensuing year a new plan of cultivation was adopted. Hitherto the land had been tilled by the community as a whole, the fields being held in common.

Now the plan was tried of allotting to each family the land which was to yield it sustenance. The result was an added acreage under cultivation, and, despite a long drought in the summer, a bountiful harvest which marked the end of Plymouth's sufferings for food.

July of 1623 brought to Plymouth the last of the Leyden brethren who were to come in a body to the new home of their church. The new-comers numbered about one hundred, and they came in the ship Anne and a small consort — the Little James. These immigrants brought with them their own provisions, so there was nothing to mar the satisfaction of the reunion. The passenger list of these vessels completes the roll of those who are properly called the Pilgrim Fathers.

In 1624 the first cattle were brought to Plymouth. Goats, swine and poultry, and possibly sheep, were already there in small numbers. This year saw also the beginning of a profitable trade with the Maine Indians on the Kennebec River which was to continue until the French seizure of Plymouth's trading post and properties in 1635. In the same year (1635) a similar fate overtook a Plymouth trading post on the Connecticut River

THE RETURN OF THE MAYFLOWER.
Permission New England Mutual Life.

— only this time the seizure was by Englishmen of Massachusetts Bay Colony.

But the most important event of this fifth year of the new Colony was the conspiracy of Oldham and Lyford against the Congregational form of church government. Oldham was one of nine "Particulars" — men who lived at Plymouth without sharing in its business responsibilities and benefits — who had come over in the Anne in 1623. Lyford was an Episcopal clergyman who had been surreptitiously smuggled into the Colony by some of the Adventurers who wished to win it over to the Church of England.

These two men with what malcontents they could win to their aid, set about organizing a rival church — in secret, of course. At the same time they wrote vilely slanderous accounts of the Pilgrim leaders to their London backers. Governor Bradford, having discovered the plot, seized Lyford's correspondence, and, after a public trial, both he and Oldham were banished from the Colony.

The affair did not end here, for it created a schism in the Adventurers company, many of whom were bitterly opposed to the Pilgrim Church. Its friends in the company, however, bought out the interests of the malcontents. In 1626 these in turn sold their right to the colonists themselves for eighteen hundred pounds. This debt was assumed by eight bondsmen for the Colony — Bradford, Standish, Allerton, Winslow, Brewster, Howland, Alden, and Prence.

Doubtless it would have been discharged in a very few years, but in a moment of sorry inspiration four Londoners — Sherly, Beauchamp, Andrews and Hatherly — were taken into partnership, fastening an incubus of dishonesty upon the company,— in Sherly, the London agent, — which delayed the final release from debt until 1646.

According to the original compact with the Adventurers, at the end of seven years the lands and common properties of the Colony were to be allotted in severalty to the colonists. This was done in 1627. There were one hundred and fifty-six men, women and children, constituting the purchasers of the Adventurers' right, to each of whom went a share.

It is probable that indentured servants and others raised the whole population of the settlement to something more than two hundred. There were but fifteen head of cattle in the Colony at the time, and in order to divide these the colonists were divided into twelve groups, or companies, to each of which was to be given the care and use of an animal for ten years, at the end of which time the original beast and one-half of her increase was to be restored to the public. This division took place on June first, 1627.

With the allotment in severalty the story of the Pilgrimage properly ends. Plymouth Colony was to continue an interesting and eventful history until its rights and its independence were finally taken away by Andros, the tyrannical consolidator of New England colonies, in 1686. But this history is but a chapter in the larger history of the state of Massachusetts. Plymouth was the first beginning of that state, but she was not long in advance of her sister settlements.

As early as 1622 rival settlers began to appear. In 1625 Salem was founded, and scattered dwellers established themselves in the neighborhood of the future Boston; while in 1627, at the time of the cattle division in the elder Colony, Endicott and Winthrop and the founders of the Bay settlement were already preparing for their journey. And thenceforth the stories of all these are closely interwrought, forming one history.

At the same time the spirit of Plymouth must

not be confounded with that of Massachusetts Bay. The Pilgrims were not Puritans. They were ever broader and more tolerant. In their church they were willing to receive the Episcopalian ministrations of Lyford and listen to the Baptist sermons of Roger Williams, their pastor from 1631 to 1633, freely and with appreciation so long as their democratic church government was not attacked.

In truth, it was in their firm adherence to the principles of democracy that the men of Plymouth most widely differed from their neighbors of Massachusetts Bay. The latter colony was in its beginning thoroughly aristocratic in temper and taste. But Plymouth and its Pilgrim founders had suffered too much for the sake of liberty to endure serfdom and caste in their political organization. And so it comes about that to this day we style the Pilgrim band the Forefathers of the Republic, and the Rock of their Landing is to us a corner-stone of freedom.

JOHN ALDEN'S BIBLE.

CHAPTER V.

JOHN ALDEN.

N the year of our Lord 1621 the Americas were the world's Outlands. To the peoples of Europe the New Land was a land of promise and sunset gold. Long before dim echoes of a world beyond the ocean, tales of a fair Vineland farther than Ultima Thule, had been brought from the country of the Norseman by chapmen and pilgrims who had them at the bearded lips of wild sea-scouts.

And long before Madoc, Prince of Wales, had heard the siren of the Western Sea. Ten long ships there were, laden with Madoc's folk. Singing they sailed from port, out past the Irish coast, to found a New Wales in the night-haunt of the sun. That was A. D. 1170, and the ten ship loads of folk were never heard from more. Afterwards Columbus sailed. And then Europe heard.

The ancient restless summons of the West which had drawn the tribes of our fathers' fathers from far Asian plateaus was heard anew in all her sea-borders. A hundred sails filled westward — the fleets of the explorers. Then a thousand — fishers' craft, trading vessels, the black corsair of the pirate. And so was begun the last great migration of the Aryan peoples, a migration which was to continue for one, two, three hundred years,— who knows how many centuries, for it is not yet at an end.

In the year 1621 a few straggling colonies had attained a timorous foothold along the eastern coast of North America. For more than a century and a quarter the New World had been known, yet its settlement was hardly begun. Money and lives had been freely expended in efforts to colonize, but a long list of failures as yet far overbalanced the three or four settlements that promised permanence and success. Of these the youngest was Plymouth.

A winter and summer were passed since the first coming. One-half of those who had set forth to hew them out homes in the wilderness were dead. But the other half and the Colony survived. There was no turning back. These were not men to change their faces from a venture either for its toil or its hunger or for death itself.

And so when, late in November of that year, the

ship Fortune hoisted her sails for the long eastern voyage to England it was not to carry discouraged remnants of a settlement, as so many a good ship had done before, but proudly to bear away the new colony's first cargo of merchandise — sassafras root and good clapboard and fur of the otter and beaver.

We may be sure that the people of Plymouth gathered at the beach to watch the vessel's departure. There were the thirty-five persons that the Fortune had brought, "most of them lusty yonge men, and many of them wild enough, who little considered whither or aboute what they wente."

Yet on this day at least they must have taken pause for serious thought, beginning to realize something of the hard significance and vast isolation of the new life. There were, again, the fifty men, women and children of the Mayflower. To them the going of the ship meant much. She was the sole link joining them to Europe and civilization, the sole tie to friends and home.

More precious than the freighting of lumber and fur were the letters she carried over sea — cargo of love and of hope and of much lasting sorrow, too, for those that waited. Doubtless, beside, there were some dark-skinned subjects of the sachem Massasoit scattered among the watchers, their impassive faces revealing no sign of the awe they must have felt at the white man's great canoe, their untaught wit failing to read them their race's doom in the shadow of the ship. And so she heaved her anchors and spread her canvas and bore away, her departure meaning to all of them more than their tongues could easily say.

There was one among the watchers to whom the going of the Fortune meant even more than to any of the others. A tall, handsome young man he was, the tallest and handsomest in the Colony. Perchance he stood a little apart from the rest,—in gray Pilgrim garb, worn with easy and unconscious grace, his head bared, the wind lightly toying the red-flaxen hair that hung down almost to the broad white collar over yet broader shoulders.

The ruddy and white complexion natural to him is tanned and browned by a year of out-door life in harsh New England weather, but tanned as it is the complexion speaks the health and strength and the vigorous youth of a man who is to live well nigh four score years and ten.

He has the straight nose and smooth brow of the pure Saxon; his mouth is a mixture of boyishness and Puritan strength, of resolution and purpose and of that delicate expressiveness native to the man of eloquent tongue; his blue eyes, keen, alert, serious, yet ever ready to smile. "John Alden, Cooper," he signs himself. And now as he watches the Fortune standing out to sea, he knows well that her departure, without him, sets a final seal to the way of his life and points its final course.

Over a year ago he embarked on the Mayflower, engaged for the years' service to the new colony. And now his year is spent and the vessel that might have borne him back to his fatherland is dropping below the sea's horizon. He has elected to cast his lot, for weal or woe, in the New World.

Wrote Governor Bradford: "John Alden was hired for a cooper, at South-Hampton, wher the ship victuled; and being a hopfull yong man, was much desired, but left to his owne liking to go or stay when he came here; but he stayed, and maryed here." It is simply said. A life's romance in a paragraph. He had elected to stay.

Yet on this November day, with his eyes on the fading sail, there must have been many a thought of the old places and the old faces in green England that he was never to see again. "Merrie Englande" she was yet in those days, and he loved her.

So the good ship's sails were hidden in a fog not the sea's and there were tears in the blue eyes.

"Are you sorry, John?"

Governor Bradford ended his laconic paragraph with the yet more laconic, "but he stayed and maryed here." It is the key and climax of the story. And here she stands beside him,—slender, vivacious, gracile as the young birch of the new shore,—dark-eyed Priscilla. She, too, has been looking toward the sea and the vanishing ship with no less feeling than his own. For it might—so little a hap might have caused it,—it might, even now, have been bearing him away from her forever. The ship seems almost cruel to her at the very thought.

If he had not known so soon,—if he had not spoken,—if he had not cared—ah, if he had not! She draws close up to him involuntarily—to make quite sure that he is really beside her, and not aboard the Fortune bound for England. And she casts a quick, shy, proud glance up into his face. And then she sees the tears in his blue eyes. And then—

"Are you sorry, John?"

Of course there could be but one answer to such a question, and he gives it with such a resounding

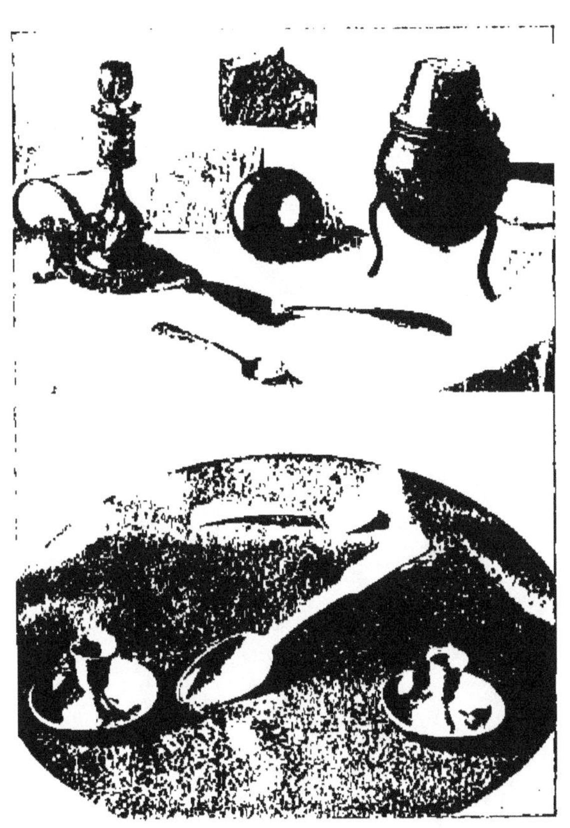

PRISCILLA'S SILVER, CANDLESTICKS AND HEATER.
(Owned by Mrs. Geo. Bolling, Brockton.)

good will that the grave elders of the Colony turn about in surprise and a certain wiry little captain, with steel morion and side arms, wheels sharply about and then as sharply back again to gaze abstractedly out to sea, the while nervously tugging at his iron-gray moustachios. But John sees nothing of all this and minds it less, and as for Priscilla — well, a kindly tan conceals her blushes.

The tears in John Alden's eyes were not tears of regret — never for a moment. He is well satisfied with his choice, and has reason to be. But there are memories of those over sea, and of the graves there,— those were honest and manly tears and no cause for shame.

The vessel disappears, and the group at the shore breaks away. But John and Priscilla do not follow toward the dozen low-eaved buildings that constitute the village.

Instead they turn toward the hillside where lies the dearest treasure that has been expended in the building of Plymouth — her dead. Among them — part of the price of the planting — are William Mullines, and his wife, and Joseph, their son,— Priscilla's all. Here they linger for a time, speaking little, for their hearts are full. Priscilla's is the young grief, but John, sober beside her, has thought of a far-away English churchyard where lie buried the generations of his fathers. He has cut loose from the old stock.

He has established a new home in the wilderness and fastened his hopes on a new land. He has taken to wife a daughter of refugees, orphaned as he is orphaned, wotting neither kith nor kin. Her health and her beauty are all her dowry — these and the cunning of her hands. But he asks no more, and he is well content to render her arm-service and heart-service, the best of his strength and love.

The lights in the windows of Plymouth are already shining when these two — well rejoiced in one another — at last turn their steps toward The Street. They have buried the dead past. Before them is the New World future. And doubt not something of the poetry and magnificence of that future, some vision of the free nation that is to be reared by their handicraft, its might and its achievement, is revealed to them.

On one side of them is the darkling sea stretching away to Europe and things gone by; but they turn instead to the shadowy, mysterious band of New England forest, nor do they feel now its awe and hidden fears, for it seems to them a forest of promise and over it falls the golden light of the sinking sun — the age-long lure of their race.

That was in 1621. In the year of our Lord 1902 the world is well nigh three hundred years older. And the old have long and troublesome memories. They delve and dig into the ashes of the past seeking some token of the dead days that are gone, if perchance they may live again. A faded, yellow scrawl, a rain-eaten date on a fallen stone, a fragment of old ware — anything that yet may bring some echo of the vanished joy into the toil of today.

Reaction from the too fevered and strained life of the Nineteenth Century has caused us to turn for rest and relief and poetry to the romance of earlier days. Then a man's hand was a man's, whether wielding musket, or oar, or hoe. Life was a battle with the Wilderness, and the toiler's wits were matched with the wiles of an upkempt Nature which it was his to shear with the axe and his to comb with the plough. Yet the toil was still not greater than its reward, and there was time for thought of the soul.

In those days no man asked concerning another, who were his sires. Each was content to accept his fellows for what they were in themselves and for what they could do — for their man-value, as the need then was. That the Fathers gave thought to the parents who had borne them over-sea, we well know, for they were reverent men. But their days were full of occupatoin, and this thought was rather the companion of plough-labor than of pen-labor; and they abode in a New World and were the beginnings of a new life, and the largeness of this, rather than remembrance of abandoned ways and places, was the theme of their speech. They remembered and held dear their house-kin in old England, as true men must, but they kept these memories sacred from profanation, deep cloistered in the heart.

Among all the Pilgrim Fathers is none whose origin is better hidden than is that of John Alden. We have the four lines of Governor Bradford's entry regarding him and we know that he was about twenty-one years old when he embarked on the Mayflower at Southampton. Beyond this nothing is certain. But there are a few facts ascertained regarding the name which warrant plausible inferences.

In mediaeval Europe surnames were by no means common properties. Among our Saxon forefathers they were not possessed even by men of rank and family, and the hero of our oldest national epic is always designated, "Beowulf, son of Ecgtheowes." With the coming of Christianity, however, came Christian baptism and the Christian name, prefixed to the epithetic or patronymic name which, in turn, developed into the surname or family name.

But the general use of surnames came about very gradually. As late as the Seventeenth and Eighteenth centuries they were still not applied to the yokel and the churl. The common name was just Tom, Dick or Harry. As time passed and the Toms, Dicks and Harrys multiplied, they were differentiated as Tom the Cooper, from Tom the Smith, Whitehead Dick from Dick the Fleet, Harry of the Dale from Harry, Harry's son; and thence very quickly arise Tom Cooper, Dick Whitehead, Harry Dale, and so on.

It is thus that names grow, and it is only in the most ancient surnames — names that have survived the wear and change of language, that we can be reasonably certain that the bearing of it is evidence of a long-established family.

Alden is such a name. It is a Teuto-Scandinavian name, being found in Holland, Germany and the Scandinavian peninsula — under such forms as

Van Alden, Aulden, and Auldine — as well as in England. This wide territorial extent alone would indicate the antiquity of the name, but it does not necessarily imply a common origin, in the stricter sense, to all who bear it. Its probable etymology, however, explains its wide extension.

The prefix "al" or "el" in Anglo-Saxon meant brave, strong, noble, illustrious,— as in Albert, "the nobly bright." "Dene" is an old spelling for the word Dane. And the meaning of Alden was, accordingly, the "brave, or noble, Dane." This does not necessarily mean that the Aldens were originally Danish, for our Saxon fathers called themselves "Danes" in early times. But it does indicate that the name was probably brought over from the Continent, and it explains, in a way, the prevalence of it in the countries bordering on the Danish peninsula — that cradle of English colonization. And it shows without question that the family was established long before the modernization of languages.

A supposition has been put forward that John Alden was an Irishman, but there are no facts to support this view. The possession of a Teutonic name is itself strong prima facie evidence to the contrary, and when the name is of as ancient formation as his there can be little doubt about the matter. But aside from the name, tradition has described John Alden as distinctively of Saxon type; and to this day his descendants almost invariably show the ethnic characteristics of that race.

An anecdote will illustrate. Mrs. Charles L. Alden of Troy, N. Y., has published the following: "My sister, while traveling there (in Norway), came across two little peasant boys; one of them resembling my little son, John Alden, she was induced to ask his name, and was startled by the reply, 'Jan Aulden'." Of course this does not mean that there was any family relationship, near or far, between young John and Jan, but it does indicate the ethnic kinship between the Scandinavian family and the Anglo-Saxon Aldens of England and America.

In England the name of Alden was widespread at the time of the Norman Conquest, A. D. 1066. In the Domesday Book — the Conqueror's census taken 1086 — Aldens and Aldenes are recorded in nearly all of the eastern counties from Hertfordshire north to York (these were the counties most affected by the Danish invasions of the Ninth Century). Many of them are entered as "tenants in capite"—that is, as holding lands directly from the King,—and manv more as having been land-holders in the time of Edward the Confessor, or the years following. Among the latter is an "Al-dene et ejus mater" of Hertfordshire, who was still, at the time of the great census, an under-holder of land. It is apparent from these records that many Aldens were men of importance and long establishment in England under the Saxon rule, but in common with the great majority of their countrymen they sank into obscurity under the despotic sway of the Norman Conqueror.

But not all branches of the family disappeared, as the recurrence of the name in later times in the ancient localities shows; nor did the Aldens wholly lose station, as is sufficiently evinced by their recorded armorial bearings, notably numerous among the Aldens of Hertfordshire.

The immediate family of the Pilgrim leader is unknown. It is hardly to be doubted that he was orphaned when he embarked for America, and it is not believed that he had either brothers or sisters. But so far as is known there was but one prominent Alden family in southern England at the time. The seat of this family was in the neighboring shires of Hertford and Cambridge. It was to John

Alden of Hertfordshire, a lawyer of the Middle Temple, that the coat of arms mentioned in Timothy Alden's American Inscriptions (Vol. IV.) was granted in 1607.

This gentleman was doubtless the head of the family, and while it is not likely that the Pilgrim John belonged to his immediate household, still it may have been to him that the latter owed the education which enabled him to serve in later years as magistrate in Plymouth Colony. Another Alden who may have been a kinsman of the American forefather is that Robert Allden who is given as one of the London merchants, known as the "Adventurers," who furnished the financial backing of the Mayflower expedition. It is not at all unlikely that to him was due John Alden's engagement as cooper for the new colony. Bradford's statement that he was hired at Southampton might be an inaccuracy. For a cooper was a legal necessity to the expedition. A Parliamentary statute of 1543 required that "whosoever shall carry Beer beyond Sea, shall find Sureties to the Customers of that Port, to bring in Clapboard meet to make so much Vessel as he shall carry forth."

Now the English contingent of the expedition had, we are told, been embarked at London, and it is quite improbable that the men who organized it would delay the engagement of a cooper, known to be necessary, until the small port of Southampton should be reached — where they might utterly fail to find a man ready to risk his life in the wilderness. It is much the more likely that Bradford first met Alden at Southampton, where he would come to attention in connection with the finding of "Sureties to the Customers of the Port"; or, it may be that it was at Southampton that Alden first embarked, having come overland from London.

John Alden did not arrogate to himself the then somewhat considerable title of "Master,"— or "Mister," as we say it. Although this title was afterward coupled with his name both by Governor Bradford and by John Winthrop, the aristocratic governor of Massachusetts Bay, still to the last he was accustomed to sign himself plain "John Alden," or, if anything more were needed, "Cooper" or "Yeoman" might be added. The yeomen of England were the descendants of the freeholders and landed gentry of pre-Norman times, and among them were many names which had stood high in the kingdom in the days before the Conquest.

The standing of a cooper, or, as then described,

an "artificer of the Mystery of Coopers," corresponded to that of the skilled mechanic or technologist of today, and denoted special training and emolument. That the Pilgrim cooper possessed a better education than even his trade required is abundantly evidenced by the forward position he immediately took in the affairs of the Colony. In days when the ability to write one's name was by no means common, he was the youngest signer of the famous Compact. Governor Bradford's note in the list of the Mayflower's passengers well signifies what station the young Alden was accorded in men's minds.

But titles meant very little in Plymouth Colony. A purer democracy in spirit or in fact has never existed than was that instituted by the framers of the Compact. Born of rebellion against the religious tyranny of the Established Church, the Christian fellowship of the Congregation and the democratic spirit of the Congregational form of church government soon tempered the whole social, political and religious life of the Pilgrim Fathers.

Long before Rousseau, they discovered and put into practice a doctrine of the rights of man, and framed an original compact of government, which should far outlast the theories of the great political philosopher.

As should be in a true democracy, the holding of office was rather an honorable burden than a titled privilege. It was a token of esteem and a tacit recognition of worth on the part of the community, but it conveyed no emolument comparable to its toils and it was not sought after. The assumption of official labors was rather looked upon as a duty which the strong owed their weaker brethren.

All of the Pilgrim leaders were called upon to render full stint of service to the Colony, but there is no record among them of so long and varied a public service as that of John Alden. As early as 1627, when he was but twenty-seven years of age, his name appears as one of the eight "Undertakers" who bought out the "Adventurers," and assumed the financial responsibilities and indebtedness of the Colony. In this we see not only the estimation placed upon young Alden by his elders, but something of his courage and enterprise as well, for the Colony was as yet by no means an assured success, and in case of its destruction, abandonment or bankruptcy each of the "Undertakers" would have been liable to the hopeless horrors of the debtors' prison as well as loss of property. Had he so chosen Alden might have found in his youth sufficient excuse for escaping a profitless and dangerous responsibility, but, as his after record shows, he was not a man to put upon others the performance of public duties. He remained one of the Colony's financial backers until the final wiping out of its debt in 1646.

In public office John Alden gave manifold service. He was many times surveyor of highways, and he also acted as agent for the Colony, in which capacity he had oversight of business affairs. His duties were not altogether "office work," for in 1634 we find record of a trip to Plymouth's trading post on the Kennebec River in charge of the public merchandise.

The year before he had been appointed a member of the board of assistants to the governor. This marked the beginning of magisterial duties which were to continue, with some interruption, until his death. From 1640 to 1650, almost continuously, he was deputy from the town of Duxbury, which he represented in the Colonial councils. In 1632, in 1634-9, and in 1650, he was assistant on the governor's board, and so continued from the latter date until his death in 1686. In 1665 he was styled "deputy governor." He was often on the council of war for the Colony, notably at the time of King Philip's War in 1667 and of the Dutch-English colonial troubles. Doubtless he took part in the military expeditions of the earlier years, as a man of his strength and adventurous dsiposition would be certain to do; and we know that in 1643 he and his sons, John, Jr., and Joseph, were enrolled among the eighty Duxbury men forming its military organization. But his talents were rather for administration than for warfare and while never shirking military responsibilties, his more eminent services to the commonwealth were civil and judicial.

That these services were esteemed by his contemporaries to be very considerable we have more than the evidence of mere praise. For the most part Plymouth officials received their pay in the consciousness of good service rendered. As the Colony grew older and financially able some monetary remuneration was attempted. In view of the fact that he had devoted the greater part of his time to public business for so many years, a special grant was made to Magistrate Alden. On the old colony records appears the following entry:

"In regard that Mr. Alden is low in his estate, and occationed to spend time att the Courts on the

Contreyes occation, and soe hath done this many yeares; the Court have alowed him a small gratuity the sume of ten pounds to bee payed by the treasurer."

CHAPTER VI.

PLYMOUTH MAGISTRATE.

THE duties of the Plymouth magistrate were varied and picturesque. To a considerable extent the infliction of punishments was subject to his own humor. An instance is the penalty inflicted in the early months of the Colony's existence upon Edward Lister and Edward Doty, the two servants of Master Steven Hopkins, for duelling with dagger and sword.

They were condemned to lie bound "neck and heels" for twenty-four hours before the governor's house — a vigil which without doubt cooled their knightly ardors. Stocks and fines were more common than jailings as the judicial reward of petty crimes and misdemeanors, and had the indubitable advantage of being less trying to the slender public purse. For more serious offenses there were whippings and banishments, and even hanging for murder. In 1657 it is recorded that one John Copeland was banished because he said that Mr. Alden shook and trembled in his knees when he was before him. Nowadays we should style the obstreperous

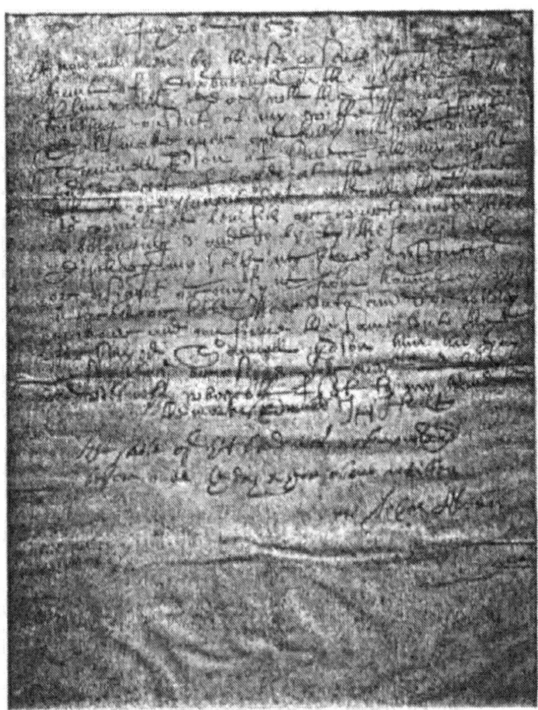

Document drawn and signed by Magistrate Alden,
Pilgrim Hall, Plymouth.

Quaker's offense "contempt of court" and give him more to think of than the privilege of farming in a frontier county.

More often, we imagine, the business of the magistrate was nothing more serious than assessment of fines for absence from church, or administering reproof to some not over-pious youngster or too tongue-loose gossip. There were the marryings, too, which were his to perform; for the Independent reaction against the Established Church went so far as to demand that the marriage ceremony be a civil and not a religious function. John Alden himself was probably married, according to this custom, by Governor Bradford; and in later years he doubtless performed the ceremony for his own as well as for his neighbors' children. We know, at least, that he married his daughter Ruth, the ancestress of the Presidents Adams, in 1657.

Of the part which John Alden played in the earliest years of the Colony's existence we have, naturally, little record. He was one of the very youngest of the men, relatively a stranger, and could hardly be looked for in places of prominence, which fell to the elders. That he took part in the first explorations is an inference necessitated by our knowledge of his fine physique. And as an experienced worker in wood he undoubtedly performed full stint in the building of Plymouth.

It is probable, too, that it was he who had supervision of the preparation of that "good clapboard" with which the Fortune was laden "as full as she could stowe" upon her return voyage in 1621; for, as we have seen, it was necessary to return to England as many prepared staves (or "clapboard" as it is called in the Parliamentary Act) as the Mayflower had carried away in her casks and tuns of ale and beer, and it was for the preparation of these that John Alden had been hired.

There is a tradition that a rivalry arose betwixt young Alden and Mary Chilton as to which should be the first to set foot on Plymouth Rock, and victory is claimed for each of them by their descendants,— so illustrious a man as John Adams upholding the claim of his Pilgrim forefather. Of course the matter can never be settled, and, indeed, would lose all interest if it could. But there are probabilities in the case, and the most pleasing of these is that both contentions spring from some fabled gallantry of Alden's. It may very likely be that John Alden was the first man and Mary Chilton the first woman to land upon the Rock on that thirty-first of January, 1621, when the Congregation held its first service on the shore. On this day it could have been small honor for a man of the Colony to be before at the landing, but a rivalry between the maids was natural enough. Nor is it likely, vigorous as the Pilgrim women were, that they would be allowed to leap from boat to shore before some muscular young man had landed with the painter and drawn the boat's nose fast nigh the landing-place. Perhaps this young man was Alden and perhaps as he helped Maid Chilton ashore he spoke some gallant phrase of the new home's welcome of the first fair foot to press its threshold — and thence sprang the tale.

In the assignment of houses and division into households in 1621, we find John Alden under the roof presided over by Captain Myles Standish, whose house was the first under Fort Hill — the captain's special charge. This is the earliest hint we have of the lifelong friendship between these two men — a friendship as romantic as that of Tristan and King Mark, or that of Siegfried and Gunther, or any other in which the hero has shown himself ready to give up the woman of his heart's choice for his friendship's sake. That the New England tale has a fairer ending than the old tragedies is altogether due to that faculty for knowing her own mind and that aptitude for expressing it which from the first has characterized the American woman.

John Alden was not a man to balk at the drivings of Fate any more than the valiant captain was a man to bear ill humor at the pranks of Cupid. He immediately set about the establishment of a new house of Alden, and in 1627, at the time of the land and cattle division, there were two American-born youngsters to be reckoned with in the distribution of acres and to share in the achievements of the red English heifer, "Raghorn."

It was not long after this that, in company with Standish and some others, the Aldens began to spend their summers on their farm at Duxbury — so called after the seat of the Standish family in England. In the Old Colony's records appears

Anº 1632 Aprell 2 — The names of those which promise to remove their families to live in the towne in the winter time, that they may the better repair to the worship of God.

And to this are appended the names of John Alden, Captain Standish, Jonathan Brewster, and Thomas Prence. But Duxbury was not long to remain a summer settlement. The causes which led to the first removal thither were such as soon to make it the permanent home of its founders. An entry in Governor Bradford's history, 1632, sets forth these causes:

"Alsoe ye people of ye plantation begane to grow in their outward estats, by reason of ye flowing of many people into ye cuntrie, espetially into ye Bay of ye Massachusets; by which means corne & cattle rose to a great prise, by wch many were much enriched, and comodities grue plentifull; and yet in other regards this benefite turned to their hurte, and this accession of strength to their weakness. For now as their stocks increased, and ye increase vendible, ther was no longer any holding them togeather, but now they must of necessitie goe to their great lots; they could not other wise keep their catle; and having oxen growne, they must have land for plowing & tillage. And no man now thought he could live, except he had catle and a great deal of ground to keep them; all striving to increase their stocks. By which means they were scatered all over ye bay, quickly, and ye towne in which they live compactly till now, was left very thine, and in a short time almost desolate. And if this had been all, it had been less, thoug to much; but ye church must also be devided, and those yt had lived so long together in Christian & comfortable fellowship must now part and suffer many divisions."

There is an odd pathos in this ancient entry. It is a sorrow for the first breaking up of the family life, the ending of the "old days"—the ten dear, toilsome years of the founding. Plymouth was like a mother parting from her first-born, and even if that parting was for the child's welfare and happiness — a marriage-parting rather than a death,— and token of a new and fruitful prosperity, still the mother-town could not lose the nurseling without some pang for the passing of the old order. Progress, like decay, brings its sadness.

John Alden's farm at Duxbury contained something more than one hundred and sixty-nine acres. It lies to the south of Blue Fish River, a runlet leading to the sea, and has long been esteemed one of the best farms of the town. The site of the Pilgrim settler's house, near Eagle Tree Pond, is now marked with a marble slab.

In Plymouth, prior to 1627, Governor Bradford, Captain Standish and Mr. Alden had been in possession of very nearly, if not quite all the land between Burial Hill and Main Street, and it was here, doubtless, neighboring Captain Standish, that the

STANDISH HOUSE, DUXBURY

Pilgrim John lived after his marriage and before his removal to Duxbury. Upon his acquisition of the Duxbury farm, however, the Plymouth property reverted to the town, and was referred to in the records as Town Common. Although for several years he was still a citizen of Plymouth, the removal to Duxbury was inevitable by reason of its distance, and, as we have seen, was accomplished in fact two or three years before the political separation.

In 1637, so it is recorded, Mr. Alden received a small addition to his farm in a hill or knoll to the north of the Blue Fish, granted "in lieu of a Pcell of land taken from him (next unto Samuel Nashes land) for publicke use." A second addition to his landed estate occurred in 1645 at Bridgewater. Bridgewater was originally a plantation granted to Duxbury in compensation for Marshfield, which was taken from her. The grant runs as follows:

"The inhabitants of the town of Duxbury are granted a competent proportion of lands about Saughtuckquett, towards the west, for a plantation for them, and to have it four miles every way from the place where they shall set up their centre: provided it intrench not upon Winnytuchquett, formerly granted to Plymouth. And we have nominated Captain Miles Standish, Mr. John Alden, George Soule, Constant Southworth, John Rogers, and William Brett, to be feofees in trust for the equal dividing and laying forth the said lands to the inhabitants."

The Bridgewater property passed into the possession of the Pilgrim's second son, Joseph, probably as his portion of the paternal estate, and allotted during his father's lifetime. The latter ended his days at Duxbury, where the greater part of his eleven children were born. The homestead was inherited by his third son Jonathan, who built the house which still stands there, and under whose roof the aged Pilgrim spent his later days.

John Alden died September twelve, 1687, in the eighty-eighth year of his age, having been born about 1599. The place of his burial is not known, but it was most likely upon a knoll in Duxbury in the southeastern part of Harden Hill. Here was the first cemetery in the town, and it was used as a burial place at least sixty years after the town's organization, and was not abandoned until several years after Mr. Alden's death.

No stones have survived the wear of the two centuries since that time, and it is much to be doubted if any were ever erected there. In the

early days all mortuary monuments were imported from England, and only at great expense, and in consequence were little used. We know beside from the annals of Plymouth that it was thought best to conceal deaths from the Indians as far as possible, and so the custom arose of not marking the last resting place of those gone upon their final pilgrimage.

At the time of his death the Pilgrim's estate inventoried only some fifty pounds sterling. But this is hardly a fair index to his actual property, as the greater portion of his possessions, including probably all his land holdings, had been deeded to his children. While he had never been a rich man, even for Plymouth Colony, he was always well-to-do, and as early as 1633 was one of the nine heaviest rated property holders of his town.

The inventory is to be found in the Plymouth County Probate Records, and like all such records of ancestral personal properties, possesses an intimate interest for all who would read in the lists of their forefathers' treasures something of the needs, the activities and the tastes of men of other days. The inventory is as follows:

The Eighth day of November 1687 Administration was Granted unto Leiutt Jonathan Alden to Administer upon

the Estate of his father Mr John Alden late of Duxbury deceased

An Inventory taken of the Estate of the late deceased Mr John Alden october 31 day 1687

	£	s	d
Neate Cattell sheep Swine & one horse	13	..	..
one Table one forme one Carpit one Cubert & coubert Cloth	..	15	..
2 Chaires	..	.3	..
bedsteds Chests & boxes	..	15	..
Andirons pot hookes and hangers	..	.8	.6
pots Tongs one quort kettle	..	10	..
by brass ware	.1	11	..
by 1 ads 1s 6d & saws 7s	..	.8	.6
by Augurs and Chisells	..	.5	..
by wedges 5s to Coupers tooles 1£ 2s	.1	.7	..
one Carpenters Joynters	..	.1	.6
Cart boults Cleavie Exseta	..	13	..
driping pan & gridirons	..	.5	..
by puter ware 1 pound 12s by old Iron 3s	.1	15	..
by 2 old guns	..	11	..
by Table linen & other linen	.1	12	..
To beding	.5	12	..
one Spitt 1s 6d & baggs 2s	..	.3	.6
one mortising axe	..	.1	..
marking Iron a Case of trenchers with other things	..	.7	..

hamen and winch exse	..	.2	.6
by one goume and a bitt of linnin Cloth	..	.7	..
by one horse bridle and Saddle liberary and Cash and weareing Clothes	18	.9	..
by other old lumber	..	15	..

Before Nathaniel Thomas Esqr Judge of the Inferior Court of Common Pleas the 8th day of November 1687 Leiut Jonathan Alden made oath that this is a true Inventory of the Estate of his father Mr John Alden deceased soe farr as he knoweth & when he knoweth more he will discover the same

Nath ll Thomas Cler.

Mr. Alden left no will, and his son Jonathan, at whose house he died, was appointed administrator of his small remaining estate, as the above entries indicate. That this office was satisfactorily fulfilled by him we have evidence in the following certification of settlement:

Wee whose names are Subscribed being personally Interested in the then Estate of John Alden senior of Duxbury Esqr lately deceased doe hereby acknowledge our selves to have Received Each of us our full Personall proportions thereof from Jonathan Alden Administrator

& thereof Doe by these prsents for our selves our heires &c Exonerate acquit & Discharge fully the said Jonathan Alden his heires &c for Ever of & from all Rights dues demands whatsoever Relateing to the aforesd Estate In Witness Whereof we have hereunto Subscribed & sealed this thirteenth day of June Ano Dom 1688. Jacobi 2dl 4to

John Alden (Seal)
Joseph Alden (Seal)
David Alden (Seal)
Prisilla Alden (Seal)
William Paybody (Seal)
Elexander Standish (Seal)
in ye Right of my wife Sarah deceased
John Bass (Seal)
in ye Right of my wife Ruth deceased
Mary Alden (Seal)
Thomas Dillano (Seal)

ALDEN HOUSE, REAR VIEW.

CHAPTER VII.

CHARACTERISTICS.

IN Bradford's Journal, year 1634, is the story of a roil in connection with Plymouth's trading post on the Kennebec River in which appears the name of John Alden. It is the one contemporary account, which has come down to us, of an adventure in which his name is to be found, and may be quoted in the governor's own quaint phraseology:

"Now it so fell out, that one Hocking, belonging to ye plantation of Pascataway, wente with a barke and comodities to trade in that river, and would needs press into their limites; and not only so, but would needs goe up ye river above their house (towards ye falls of ye river), and intercept the trade that should come to them.

"He that was cheefe of ye place forbad them, and prayed him that he would not offer them that injurie, nor goe aboute to infring their liberties, which had cost them so dear. But he answered he would goe up and trade ther in despite of them, and lye ther as longe as he pleased.

"The other tould him he must then be forced to remove him from thence, or make seasure of him if he could. He bid him doe his worste, and so wente up, and anchored ther. The other tooke a boat & some men & went up to him, when he saw his time, and againe entreated him to departe by what perswasion he could.

"But all in vaine: he could gett nothing of him but ill words. So he considered that now was ye season for trade to come downe, and if he should suffer him to lye, & take it from them, all their former charge would be lost, and they had better throw up all. So, consulting with his men, (who were willing thertoe,) he resolved to put him from his anchores, and let him drive downe ye river with ye streame; but comanded ye men yt none should shoote a shote upon any occasion, except he comanded them. He spoake to him againe, but all in vaine; then he sente a cuple in a canow to cutt his cable, the which one of them performes; but Hocking taks up a pece which he had layed ready, and as ye barke shered by ye canow, he shote him close under her side, in ye head, (as I take it,) so he fell downe dead instantly.

"One of his fellows (that loved him well) could not hold, but with a muskett shot Hocking, who fell down dead and never speake word. This was ye truth of ye thing. The rest of ye men carried home the vessell and ye sad tidings of these things. Now ye Lord Saye & ye Lord Brooks, with some other great persons, had a hand in this plantation; they write home to them, as much as they could to exasperate them in ye matter, leaving out all ye circumstances, as if he had been kild without any offenc of his parte, conceling yt he had kild another first, and ye just occasion that he had given in offering such wrong; at which their Lordsps were much offended, till they were truly informed of ye mater.

"The bruite of this was quickly carried all aboute, (and yt in ye worst maner,) and came into ye Bay to their neighbours their. Their owne barke coming home, and bringing a true relation of ye matter, sundry were sadly affected with ye thing, as they had cause. It was not long before they had occasion to send their vessell into ye Bay of ye Massachusetts; but they were so prepossesst with this matter, and affected with ye same, as they comited Mr. Alden to prison, who was in ye bark, and had been at Kenebeck, but was no actore in ye business, but wente to carie them supply. They dismist ye barke aboute her bussines, but kept him for some time. This was thought strang here, and they sente Capten Standish to give them true information, (together with their letters,) and ye best satisfaction they could, and to procure Mr. Alden's release."

Captain Standish fulfilled his mission and procured his friend's release, but only by suffering himself to be bound over to the Bay Colony's court to vouch for the truth of his relation and the genuineness of Plymouth's patent of jurisdiction over the Kennebec region. This high-handed procedure on the part of Massachusetts justly angered the authorities of her sister colony, and a sharp correspondence ensued before the affair was finally smoothed over in face of an attack in England upon colonial liberties, which compelled them all to stand together.

But as Governor Bradford adds, "they conceived they were unjustly injured, and provoked to what was done; and that their neighbors (haveing no jurisdiction over them) did more than was mete, thus to imprison one of theirs, and bind them to their courte."

In estimating the character of Pilgrim Alden one is struck, first of all, as in the case of so many other of the founders of the American nation, with the many-sidedness of his interest and achievement. He was master-mechanic, a farmer, a soldier, probably a sailor, a magistrate, a man of affairs. To be sure no one of these professions, then demanded complex training or great learning as in modern times. This was so even in England, and much more in the little settlement clinging to the hem of the wilderness.

In such a community versatility was necessarily the prime requisite of success — far more essential than great proficiency in one branch of achievement coupled with ineptitude in others. The colonization of America, and above all of New England, was an effort to transplant full-blown the civilization which in Europe was the heritage of centuries of slow growth. The many sides of that civilization, its civic and religious duties, its long-established customs, were all to be included in the activities of the new plantation, its sprout and offshoot.

But there was, beside, a wilderness to conquer, and all too few hands for its rough labors. Naturally under such circumstances the type of settler most in need and demand was the man of many skills, the man of ready hand and adaptive mind. Such an one, if he had also stout heart and hopeful spirit, would be drawn as by a magnet to the venture, finding there the proper field for his talents. John Alden was so drawn.

It was not chance or fate that made him a Pilgrim fighter of the wilds; it was his native fitness for the work. And to him and the many others of his kind,— the apt and the ready,— is very properly ascribed the beginning of the American people. They were fated to be the forefathers of a race whose versatile genius should be the marvel of mankind; for to this end they were chosen by Nature who created them true Americans even before their feet had turned aside from the green meadows of old England.

Tradition represents John Alden as a man of fine physique, as, indeed, must have been all who survived the ravages of the terrible first winter. He was said to be the tallest man in the colony, and the handsomest. We know that he outlived all of his grown comrades of the Mayflower company, save only one or two of the girls, and this alone speaks well for his strength and vitality. He has proven, beside, father of a long-lived race.

His character, we are told, was gentle and faithful, as a strong man's should be. He was much commended for his piety and Godliness, too, and

Snow-shoe given John Alden by the Indians.
Halberd from cellar of Alden House ; in Pilgrim Hall, Plymouth
John Alden's Signature.

his ancient Bible, preserved in Pilgrim Hall, bears still the pious token of his thumb. In England he was most likely a Puritan, but in Plymouth and Duxbury he was identified with the Congregationalist Church of the Pilgrims.

An eloquent tongue is another trait in which he foreshadowed an American characteristic; and he is said to have been fond of military ways — a taste which was to find fuller expression among his descendants. But perhaps the last word which is to be spoken — the key to his personality — is the first which we have recorded. He was a "hopfull yonge man, and was much desired."

Index of finer character could not be found, for hopefulness amid the sickness and death of that dread first season was not a quality like to live in any save a blithe and tender heart, and we may well believe that finding in him a spirit of cheer the weary Pilgrims were wistful of his stay.

In certain quarters John Alden has been criticised because he countenanced the laws which Plymouth enacted against the Quakers, and, in his capacity of magistrate, executed them. Such criticism is unjust. As magistrate it was his duty to carry out the law, and the statutes themselves, which, no doubt, he helped to frame, were neither severe nor actuated by a spirit of intolerance. The Quaker craze — it can be termed no less — which swept over New England in the fifties of the Seventeenth century stood for principles not unlike those of the anarchy of the present day.

The Quakers were almost invariably eloquent scolds, and they deemed it their mission to outrage the sense of decency, insult the religion, and defy the laws of the communities in which they lived. It was for what we term misdemeanors, and not for their religious opinions that the Quakers were punished. Their offences were against civil law. The severest penalty which Plymouth inflicted upon them was banishment; and this, in those days, meant little more than the procedure so common in country districts in our own day, of advising the unruly citizen to "move on." Generally peaceful isolation little suited the proselyting spirit of the religious reformer, and he would return again to challenge the ways of the community he had outraged, and occasionally upon a too obstreperous return was whipped for his temerity.

It is not to be wondered at that the spirit of Plymouth should have been roused against those who sought, as the early Quakers undoubtedly did seek, to create dissension and division in the church fellowship which her founders had crossed the sea to preserve and expended such price of labor and life to nurture in freedom and peace. And yet there is evidence enough that the Old Colony was not over-harsh.

Surely the proclamation of a day of prayer and fasting to beseech of the Lord deliverance from drought and Indians, and from "the scourge of Quakers," speaks more of long-suffering and patience under affliction than of malevolent intolerance. And runs an ancient entry of 1660: "Whereas there is a constant monthly meeting of Quakers from Divers places in great numbers, which is very offensive and may prove greatly prejudicial to the government, and as the most constant place for such meetings is at Duxbury, the Court have desired and appointed C. Southworth and W. Pabodie to repair to such meetings, together with the marshal or constable of the town, and to use their best endeavors, by argument and discourse, to convince or hinder them."

Perhaps the best vindication, if any were needed for Magistrate Alden's sentencings, is to be taken from the mouth of one who suffered at the hand of the court in which he sat. In 1657 a Quaker named Humphrey Norton, — who was probably insane, for he claimed to be a prophet,— addressed abusive letters to members of the court that had banished him.

And one of them began: "John Alden, I have weighed thy waies, and thou art like one fallen from thy first love; a tenderness once I did see in thee and moderation to act like a sober man; which through evill councell and selfe love thou art drawn aside from." That the letter continues with abuse, matters little. The man was crazed, and he believed himself persecuted. But even so, we have his gracious phrase — "a tenderness once I did see in thee and moderation." With this and with Bradford's gentle words we may be sure that we have the characteristics that made the youth one "much desired" — the moderation and tenderness and hopefulness of the most loveable of the Pilgrim Fathers.

There is an old-time elegy by the Reverend John Cotton "on the death of the honourable John Alden, for many years magistrate of Old Plymouth," with which it is ever fitting to close memoir of him:

The staff of bread, and water eke the stay,
From sinning Judah God will take away;

The prudent counsellor, the honorable,
Whom grace and holiness makes delectable,
The judge, the prophet, and the ancient saint;
The deaths of such cause sorrowful complaint.
The earth and its inhabitants do fall,
The aged saint bears up its pillars all.
The hoary head in way of righteousness
A crown of glory is. Who can express
Th' abundant blessings by disciples old!
In every deed they're more than can be told.
The guise 'tis of a wanton generation
To wish the aged soon might quit their station,
Though truth it be, the Lord our God does frown,
When aged saints by death do tumble down.
What though there be not such activity,
Yet in their prayers there's such fervency
As doth great mercy for a place obtain,
And gracious presence of the Lord maintain.
Though nature's strength in old age doth decay,
Yet the inward man renew'd is day by day.
The very presence of a saint in years,
Who lifts his soul to God with pray'rs and tears.
Is a rich blessing unto any place,
Who have that mercy to behold his face.
When sin is ripe and calls for desolation
God will call home old saints from such a nation.

Let sinners then of th' aged weary be.
God give me grace to mourn most heartily
For death of this dear servant of the Lord,
Whose life God did to us so long afford.
God lent his life to greater length of days;
In which he liv'd to his Redeemer's praise.
In youthful time he made Moses his choice,
His soul obeying great Jehovah's voice,
Freely forsook the world for sake of God,
In his house with his saints to have abode.
He followed God into this wilderness;
Thereby to all the world he did profess,
Affliction with his saints a better part
And more delightful to his holy heart,
Than sinful pleasures, lasting but a season.
Thus said his faith, so saith not carnal reason.
He came one of the first into this land,
And here was kept by God's most gracious hand
Years sixty-seven, which time he did behold
To poor New England mercies manifold.
All God's great works to this his Israel
From first implanting that to them befell;
Of them he made a serious observation,
And could of them present a large narration.
His walk was holy, humble, and sincere,
His heart was filled with Jehovah's fear,

He honour'd God with much integrity,
God therefore did him truly magnify,
The heart of saints entirely did him love,
His uprightness so highly did approve,
That whilst to choose they had their liberty
Within the limits of this Colony,
Their civil leader, him they ever chose.
His faithfulness made hearts with him to close.
With all the governours he did assist;
His name recorded is within the list
Of Plymouth's pillars to his dying day.
His name is precious to eternal day.
He set his love on God and knew his name,
God therefore gives him everlasting fame.
So good and heav'nly was his conversation,
God gave long life, and show'd him his salvation.
His work now finished upon this earth;
Seeing the death of what he saw the birth,
His gracious Lord from heaven calls him home
And saith, my servant, now to heaven come;
Thou hast done good, been faithful unto me,
Now shalt thou live in bliss eternally.
On dying bed his ails were very great,
Yet verily his heart on God was set.
He bare his griefs with faith and patience,
And did maintain his lively confidence;

Saying to some, the work, which God begun,
He would preserve to its perfection.
His mouth was full of blessings till his death
To ministers and Christians all; his breath
Was very sweet by many a precious word
He utter'd from the spirit of his Lord,
He liv'd in Christ, in Jesus now he sleeps;
And his blest soul the Lord in safety keeps.

JOHN ALDEN, Anagram, END AL ON HI.

Death puts an end to all this world enjoys,
And frees the saints from all, that here annoys.
This blessed saint has seen an end of all
Worldly perfections. Now his Lord doth call
Him to ascend from earth to heaven high,
Where he is blessed to all eternity.
Who walk with God as he, shall so be blessed,
And evermore in Christ his arms shall rest.
Lord, spare thy remnant, do not us forsake,
From us do not thy holy spirit take.
Thy cause, thy int'rest in this land still own
Thy gracious presence ay let be our own.

John Alden's Chair (owned by Mrs. Geo. Bolling, Brockton, Mass.)
Cabinet brought from England by John Alden, (owned by Wm. H. Alden, Lansdowne, Pa.)

CHAPTER VIII.

THE DAUGHTER OF THE NORMAN.

IT was a fair day to live — that fourteenth day of October, Anno Domini 1066. The harvest was gathered and the sweetness and spice of autumn was in all the mellow air. There were deer for the price of a bow-shot in the glades of the changing forest, and the sun-flecked meadows and hill-slopes were pleasant to the eye.

Yes, it was a fair day for living yonder in Sussex nigh to the town of Hastings, but a fair day for dying, too, when the death was to be for the fatherland and the hearthside or yet for leal love of gallant lord, for God's cause, and salvation. And if it were well to die for these things, so were there many stout carls and many brave earls, and knights and squires not a few fated to know that weal on that day.

There was a hill-crest and a breastwork of wattling and staves and serried ranks of Saxon axemen biding the onslaught. High above them floated the golden and jewelled banner of Harold the King, bravest and noblest of the rulers of Britain since the great Alfred had been laid away.

Athwart the fields another banner was advancing, borne by the good Knight Tosteins Fitz-Rou le Blanc, the banner consecrated and blessed by the Pope — for this was a holy cause which was bringing the Norman invader into England. While the Confessor was yet alive, Harold had visited Normandy, and there Duke William had forced him to swear a great oath, over the bones of saints, that William should be king of England when Edward died. And however extorted, such an oath was sacred and not lightly to be cast aside. So all over Europe the clergy had proclaimed William's war a holy war, and the Pope had blessed and consecrated the banner that should lead to victory. And now it was being borne forward by the good Knight Tosteins Fitz-Rou le Blanc, and with it were advancing fifty thousand knights of Normandy and France, and of squires and men-at-arms ten thousand more. Before all that host rode Taillefer, the lutesman, singing the ancient Chanson de Roland, the prowess and chivalry of the great Knights Paladin.

The day before there had come to the Saxon camp a monk called Hugues Maigrot bringing from William a message: "Go and tell Harold that if he will keep his former compact with me, I will leave him all the country which is beyond the Humber, and will give his brother Gurth all the lands which Godwin held. If he still persist in refusing my offers, then thou shalt tell him, before all his people, that he is a perjurer and a liar, that he and all who shall support him are excommunicated by the mouth of the Pope, and that the bull to that effect is in my hands."

At the dread word, "excommunicated," the English Aethelings turned pale. Yet they were men who loved their homes more than they feared hell, and one of them spoke for his fellows: "We must fight, whatever may be the danger to us; for what we have to consider is not whether we shall accept and receive a new lord, as if our king were dead; the case is quite otherwise. The Norman has given our lands to his captains, to his knights, to all his people, the greater part of whom have already done homage to him for them. They will all look for their gift if their Duke become our King; and he himself is bound to deliver up to them our goods, our wives, and our daughters; all is promised to them beforehand. They come, not only to ruin us, but to ruin our descendants also, and to take from us the country of our ancestors.

"And what shall we do, whither shall we go, when we have no longer a country?" It is little strange that they chose to fight for their own, — even though the numbers of their foemen far exceeded theirs; even though they were weakened and sore and wounded from the just-fought battle against another invader, Hardrada of Norway; aye, even though hell yawned to receive them dead — for that was what to them meant the Pope's excommunication.

The battle was opened by that same Taillefer, the lutesman. Wrote the old chronicler: "And when they drew nigh to the English, 'A boon, sire!' cried Taillefer. 'I have long served you, and you owe me for all such service. Today, so please you, you shall repay it. I ask as my guerdon, and I beseech you for it earnestly, that you will allow me to strike the first blow in the battle!' And the Duke answered: 'I grant it.' Then Taillefer put his horse to gallop, charging before all the rest, and struck an Englishman dead, driving his lance below the breast into his body, and stretching him upon the ground. Then he drew his sword and struck another, crying out: 'Come on, come on! What do ye sirs? Lay on, lay on!' And at the second blow he struck the English, pushed forward and surrounded and slew him. Forthwith arose the noise and cry of war, and on either side the people put themselves in motion. The Normans moved on to the assault, and the English defended themselves well. Some were striking, others urging onward, all were bold and cast aside fear. And now, behold, that battle was gathered whereof the fame is yet mighty. Loud and far resounded the bray of the horns and the shock of the lances, the mighty strokes of maces and the quick clashing of swords."

So was begun the memorable battle of Hastings. Long hours of fighting followed. The Normans charged again and again, but the English defended sturdily and beat them back, ofttimes with much slaughter. Harold's men were for the most part armed with great two-handed battle-axes, and for defense they bore long shields. They were drawn up in a solid wedge before their fortifications, and against their tight-closed ranks the Norman lancers hurled themselves in vain.

Neither could Duke William's archers effect any great damage, for the long shields defended well. As the day wore on the Normans advanced beyond a fosse, or ditch, in the midst of the plain, "having passed it in the fight without regarding it," as the chronicler tells us. "But the English charged and drove the Normans before them till they made them fall back upon this fosse, overthrowing into it horses and men. Many were to be seen falling therein, rolling one over the other, with their faces to the earth, unable to rise. . . . At no time during the day's battle did so many Normans die as perished in that fosse."

It was then that the day seemed lost to the Normans, but the Conqueror was a leader of wit. He bade his bowmen shoot their arrows up into the air, so that falling they would strike the English in their faces. And Harold's men, not daring to break their closed ranks lest they be overborne by the Norman cavalry, formed only too admirable a target for this archery. Fate feathered the shafts. Among the first struck was King Harold, a Norman arrow putting out his eye. In his agony he could no longer keep wary watch over his men. The Normans charged and again fell back; but this retreat was a ruse to draw the English in pursuit. "Like fools they broke their lines and pursued." Harold had not allowed this, but Harold was blinded. The Normans turned on their pursuers, and this time their charge bore them even to the golden and jewelled banner of the Saxons and to the King there. He died fighting, and with him fought and died the bravest Thanes of his realm.

"The English were in great trouble at having lost their King, and at the Duke's having conquered their standard; but still they fought on, and defended themselves long, and in fact till the day drew to a close. Then it clearly appeared to all that the standard was lost, and the news had spread throughout the army that Harold, for certain, was dead, and all saw that there was no longer any hope, so they left the field, and those fled who could."

Thus ended the first eventful meeting of Norman and Saxon in the battle which gave England into the hands of the invader, and despoiled her ancient families of their heritage. The boding words of the Saxon Thane who answered Hugues Maigrot on the day before the battle proved all too true a prophecy. Into the keep of the Normans — and none too gentle a keeping it was — were delivered the wives and the daughters and the houses and the goods of the conquered people, and strangers became lords in the land.

King Harold's army was largely made up of men

from the southern and eastern counties of his domain. To quote once more the Norman chronicler: "Harold had summoned his men, earls, barons and vavasors, from the castles and the cities, from the ports, the villages and the boroughs. . . . Those of London had come at once, and those of Kent, of Hertfort and of Essesse, those of Suree and Sussesse, of St. Edmund and Sufoc, of Norwis and Norfoc, of Cantorbierre and Stanfort, Bedefort and Hundetone," and so it continues.

Every man who could bear arms and had heard the war-call was in the ranks — if an Earl or a Thane, armed with buckler and axe and the short Saxon sword; if yeoman or carl, armed with scythe or pick or stave, whatever weapon lay readymost. Among them there was more than one Alden, for the name was common among the freeholders of the counties whence the army came.

And with the men "of Hertfort" it is hard to believe that that "Aldene" who held land from Edward the Confessor was not to be found — he and his father, too, as their duty was, fighting for hearth and home, for wife and mother, under the blazoned banner of King Harold. Only when the last vengeful stand of the Saxons at the edge of the forest wreaked parting vengeance on the pursuing

Normans (William of Poictiers tells us of it), the father was no longer with the son, but lay out on the hill-slope, stark with his King. And so it came about ten years later when the great census was taken that the scribe entered only "Aldene at ejus mater" — Alden and his mother. That fourteenth day of October, in the year 1066, was the beginning of dark years for his race.

But for the henchmen of William the Conqueror the day's battle meant something far other. For them it meant the beginning of a life of luxury and culture, of knightly chivalry decked in all the splendor Saxon wealth could buy. Among them was one Richard de Molinelles — so called from the ville and castle of Molinelles, or Molineux, in Normandy, which was built by Robert, surnamed "le Diable."

And it is from this Norman family of Molinelles, or Molyneux, or Molines, as it is variously called, that are descended the English families of Molineux and Molyns and Mullens, and their French cousins, the Moulins and Molines. And to one of them, William Molines, or Mullins, as he came to be called, was born not far from the year 1600 a daughter, whom he named Priscilla, after that Priscilla Paul abode with in Corinth.

History tells strange coincidences, and time works strange reconciliations. Five centuries and a half after the battle of Hastings, Saxon and Norman, an Alden and a Molines, again meet. But this time both are borne in the invader's vessel, and the battle that they are to fight will be fought standing side by side, for it is a battle to conquer a wilderness and to establish their mingled blood in a new land.

When early in the Eleventh century Robert le Diable built his castle on the banks of the Seine, he called it Molyneux — "the Mill on the Waters" — perhaps from some ancient mill located there. From this Robert sprang two families which took their names from the ancient water-mill. That Richard de Molinelles who followed his Norman Duke to England acquired from Roger de Poitou an estate in Lancashire, and thence through Adam de Molinaus (temp. Stephen, Rex), and his grandson Richard came the English Earls of Sefton, and the baronial families of Molyneux and Molines, and many heads of manors bearing some spelling of the ancient name.

But in Normandy the original family still continued. In the year 1198 William de Molines built anew the castle Molyneux, and long after that time the "des Moulins," as they came to be called, were prominent among the gentle families of Normandy.

It is difficult to say whether William Molines, the father of Priscilla, came from the French or from the English branch of the family. There are facts pointing in each direction. The name, as we have seen, might be either French or English, and the same, oddily enough, may be said of all the Christian names that have come down to us in William Molines' immediate family. Griffis and Baird say that Mr. Molines was with the Pilgrims at Leyden, and with his family embarked on the Speedwell at Delfthaven, and we know that a Walloon, or French-Protestant Church was established at Leyden long before the Scrooby Congregation arrived there; and, from the Dutch marriage records, that there were Molines among them.

Through Winslow and others we learn that several of the French joined themselves to the Pilgrim Church. All of this tends to support the generally accepted tradition that William Molines and his family were French Hugenots. But from Mr. Molines will we learn that he had a married daughter in England, and presumably a son and property there; and this seems to point to an English birth and residence. And yet the daughter lived, and the will was proved in the county of Surrey, far to the south of the district whence the Pilgrims made their way to Holland, where we first find William Molines.

It seems evident enough that his going to Leyden was independent of theirs, and as he was a man of some property it is hard to believe that he would have abandoned an estate in England, without reason, to live in war-threatened Holland. It may be, therefore, that he was one of the French Hugenots in Leyden at the time of the arrival of the refugees from Scrooby, and that, with others of his nation, he joined their congregation there.

The daughter Sarah, who lived in Surrey, may very well have married one of the English soldiers in Holland, who, having some estate in England (for why should her father leave her but ten shillings except she were already better provided for than his other children?) and no leaning toward Congregationalism, took her home with him to live. And in their charge may have been left Mr. Molines' eldest son and such goods as he chose not to take with him when he cast in his lot with the emigrants to America.

The Huguenots were to France what the Puritans were to England. They were Protestant rebels against Romanism and against the corruption of the established church. But reformation found a less congenial soil across the channel. There were long series of persecutions culminating in the terrible massacre of St. Bartholomew's day; and so it came to pass that the French Protestants were made wanderers upon the face of the earth.

Many of them fled to England, and many to Holland, where for the most part they joined the congregations of their kinsmen the Walloons, driven from Belgium by the Spanish Inquisition. As early as 1584 a Walloon church had been formed at Leyden, and in the congregation were included many nobles and scholars as well as artisans, from France and from the Catholic provinces of the Netherlands.

When Robinsin's congregation arrived, the Dutch authorities granted them together with their French co-religionists the use of the church called St. Catharine Gasthuis. Thus from the very first there was much intercourse between the two nationalities. Several of the English as we know, and among them Bradford, were apprenticed to French weavers. Several of the French, on the other hand, joined the English Church, and when the emigration to America was projected attached themselves to the company.

We know little enough about the Pilgrims Molines. They bore an ancient and aristocratic name, and the father was a man of culture, and, for the times and in view of the circumstances, the possessor of a not inconsiderable property. He was accorded the title of "Master" in Bradford's entries. As to what his business was in Leyden we can only offer a conjecture from the stock of boots and shoes which he carried with him to the New World, as mentioned in his will. This will, in fact, tells us the most of his history that we know, for he died early in that first dire winter, on February twenty-one, 1621. The will is dated April two, but this is doubtless the date when the certified copy was signed. In the old records it is given as follows:

2: April 1621

In the name of God Amen: I comit my soule to God that gave it and my bodie to the earth from whence it came. Alsoe I give my goodes as followeth That fforty poundes in the hand of goodman Woodes I give my wife tenn poundes, my sonn Joseph tenn poundes, my daughter Priscilla tenn poundes, and my eldest sonne tenn poundes. Alsoe

I give to my eldest sonne all my debtes, bonds, bills (onelye yt forty poundes excepted in the handes of goodman Wood) given as aforesaid wth all the stock in his owne handes. To my eldest daughter I give ten shillings to be paid out of my sonnes stock. Furthermore that goodes I have in Virginia as followeth To my wife Alice halfe my goodes & to Joseph and Priscilla the other halfe, equallie to be devided betweene them. Alsoe I have xxj dozen of shoes, and thirteene paire of bootes wch I give into the Companies handes for forty poundes at seaven yeares and if they like them at that rate. If it be thought to deare as my Overseers shall thinck good And if they like them at that rate at the divident I shall have nyne shares whereof I give as followeth twoe to my wife, twoe to my sonne William, twoe to my sonne Joseph, twoe to my daughter Priscilla, and one to the Companie. Allsoe if my sonne William will come to Virginia I give him my share of land furdermore I give to my twoe Overseers Mr John Carver and Mr Williamson, twentye shillings apeece to see this my will performed desiringe them that he would have an eye over my wife and children to be as fathers and friendes to them; Allsoe to have a speciall eye to my man Robert wch hathe not so approved himselfe as I would he should have done.

This is a Coppye of Mr Mullens his Will of all particulars he hathe given. In witness whereof I have sett my hande

John Carver, Giles Heale, Christopher Joanes.

Vicesimo tertio: die mensis Julii Anno Domini Millesimo sexcentesimo vicesimo primo Emanavit Commissio Sare Blunden als Mullins filie naturali et legitime dicti defuncti ad administrand bona iura et credita eiusdem defuncti iuxta tenorem et effectum testamenti suprascripti eo quod nullum in eodem testamento nominavit executorem de bene etc Jurat.

(On the twenty-third day of the month of July, Anno Domini 1621, issued a commission to Sarah Blunden, formerly Mullins, natural and legitimate daughter of the said deceased, for administering the goods, rights and credits of the deceased, according to the tenor and effect of the above-written testament, inasmuch as he named no executor in that testament. In due form &c swears.)

This will was proved in Dorking, in county Surrey, on the date above given. It is evident that William Molines, Sr., died on board the Mayflower, for the two witnesses of the will besides Governor Carver, who doubtless drew it up, are Giles Heales and Christopher Joanes — the surgeon and the captain of that vessel. He died, too, little witting how soon his wife and his son Joseph were to follow him.

Concerning these, or the dates of their deaths, we have nothing more than Bradford's ever laconic paragraph: "Mr. Molines, and his wife, his sone, and his servant, dyed the first winter." Let us hope for poor Robert Carter, the servant, that in death, at least, he so approved himself as his master might wish.

That was a sad first winter for the maiden Priscilla. Father, mother and brother, one by one, were laid at rest on the little knoll by the seaside and their graves were levelled over, as if they were not, so that no man might know where the resting-place was or disturb them in their long sleep. And wheat was sown there — wheat whereof the grain was never to be reaped; which, when the spring came, covered with tender and velvety green the burial goal of their Pilgrimage.

Well, it was something that they lay not beneath the chill waters of the gray Northern sea; that they had seen the promised land ere their eyes forever closed, and had touched it ere the last long numbness deadened touch once for all; that they had chosen and made it their home in death. Oh, those graves there, on the little knoll by the sea-side, were strong, strong fetters to bind the feet of the living fast to that land! And the dead — were not the dead pledge and hostage stronger to hold them than grants and patents of kings? Sacred pledge, precious hostage, final surety that that Pilgrim band would not turn their faces from the way they had set!

And the Huguenot maiden Priscilla — in a strange, wild land, amid a people not her own, heartsick and homesick and weary. Yet she, too, had given her pledges — more nobly than ever gave knightly sire his own. Yonder beneath the greening wheat they lay, and the thought of them bound and held her steadfast.

Yet was there many a day of that springtide, herself but half-awakened from the winter's night-mare, when her heart turned yearning to the brother and sister still beyond the sea, and her eyes were fain to behold the gay tulip beds of Holland or yet the sunny slopes of la belle France, glorious as ever the wistful imagination of the exile's daughter might paint her Patrie. And on such days, it may be, she felt the tender, silent sympathy of the fair-haired Saxon youth, and yielded herself to its gracious comfort with all the abandonment of the sick heart — nor knew yet that she loved.

But there were other eyes that beheld her sorrowing, and pitied with that soft pity of gentlest kin. So it came to pass one sunny day that the Saxon youth came to her, with eloquent tongue but pallid lips, to do his friend's errand. He had conquered once — conquered invading jealousy and self-desire, and had buried them in the narrow confines of the heart's charnel, even as King Harold had conquered the Norseman and buried him in his "seven feet of English soil." But the harder battle with the Norman was yet to be fought, and the maid bore a banner not lightly to be withstood, for it was concentrated by love.

Yet he battled well and spoke as a true Aetheling for his friend. Perhaps he had won the day had the god of war prevailed — for was she not but a frail, strange maid, this Norman foe? But a gentler deity had charge over the issue, and so when the time came, from a bow which was the ruby bow of a demoiselle's lips, he sped the fateful dart. We all know it, how swift it flew and true — "Prithee, why don't you speak for yourself, good Master

John?" Another Harold was blinded, and another Hastings won.

"And seeing it hath pleased Him to give me to see thirty years compleated since these beginnings; and that the great works of His Providence are to be observed, I have thought it not unworthy my paines to take a view of the decreasings and increasings of these persons, and such changes as hath pased over them and theirs in this thirty years."

Thus wrote Governor Bradford in the year 1650, as he was about to add the last lines to his ever famous Journal. Of one entry I have already quoted part: "Mr. Molines, and his wife, his sone and his servant dyed the first winter." To this part should be added: "Only his dougter Priscila survied and married with John Alden, who are both living, and have 11 children. And their eldest daughter is married, and hath five children."

Of the life of Priscilla, save that she shared the life of her husband, and was the mother of children, we know little, indeed. Yet is there no necessity for knowing the count and tale of her daily duties. For we can picture the home-warding from ancient scenes and furnitures and the old ways as tradition tells them. And for the rest — what she was as a woman and what her life meant — we may well judge from what her children were; for after all a mother's children are her best biography. Of these we know that they were men and women honorable and honored, brave and chivalrous and open-hearted, a comfort to their mother's eyes.

When Priscilla died is not known, nor where she was buried, though doubtless this was nigh where her husband was afterwards laid. Let us hope that she abode with him until his years were well worn away, and was one of those "twelfe persons liveing of the old stock this present yeare, 1679" as is added, in another hand than Bradford's, beneath the lines where he had last laid aside his pen twenty years before.

For us of the present day Priscilla will ever remain the maiden of that first eventful year — she whose beauty and wit have been the tradition of our earliest years, the charm and romance of our youth, and the sunny solace of our graying years. She will ever remain the Priscilla that inspired the sweetest idyl from the pen of that poet, who but for her would never have seen light of day to lighten with his songs the days of others, his countrymen and hers, — for she, too, was American.

CHAPTER IX.

THE WOOING OF PRISCILLA.

THE story itself is simple enough, and as handed down to us, bare of adornment, it is almost archaic in its directness and point. In the traditional form it is just the naked scaffolding of a true-love tale, but withal a scaffold so firm and substantial, so honestly grounded in the enduring basis of human nature, that it has served long and well to trellis the fair foliage and fragrant flowering of romance with which the fancies of poet and novelist have so effectually adorned it.

For, indeed, it takes little in the way of fact to serve the poet's need where the tale to be told is the world-ancient story of "a young man's way with a maid" (though here, perchance, the phrase should be reversed). Just as the scientist reconstructs an extinct fish from a single scale or an ancient mammal from a chance-kept bone, so the poet taking the merest hint of an old-time romance, clothes it with the flesh and blood which his imagination creates — which we, beholding, are persuaded must be its true form and substance.

PRISCILLA AT HER WHEEL

Now there are certain sour historians — degenerate successors of Father Herodotus, always ready to tell a good story in default of a fact, — who come, unimpeachably armed with their canons of evidence, to inform us that the story of the wooing of Priscilla cannot be accepted as more than ancient gossip until it presents better credentials than the "handed down by tradition," which satisfied our uncritical fathers.

Most of us are content to take it as gossip — an unusually choice bit, too, — and to repeat it with no less relish on that account; for whether it is true in the way the sour historians demand or not, we are all very sure that it is "good enough to be true." Indeed, it is too good not to be true and for its own sake deserves to be believed, — as it has been, and is, and is likely to continue to be believed, despite the canons of evidence. And after all its credentials are not so bad. Its one fault under the learned lenses, is that it has not been proven true; but quite as surely it has never been proven false. "Handed down by tradition" may not suit the needs of the man of tomes and vellums, but for us of happy credulity the warrant is sound. And reflect, kind reader, that it is a warrant quite as good as the "handed down in the family," which establishes the character of the grandfather's clock, or the old pewter trencher left you as a great-aunt's legacy.

Like the clock and the trencher the tale exists. It is just as much a part of your family furnishing, just as much an heirloom as are they; and as with them, its existence must somehow or other be accounted for. What better or likelier origin shall we find than the traditional one?

There was a time, ere the guile of printer's ink had become of common notoriety, when to have "seen it in print" was sufficient to establish any story's reputation. And even yet we are inclined to credit the printing, yellow and venerable with age, which we know to have been implicitly believed in its day, and to have been written and printed to be believed.

Perhaps the fact of the long belief which, like a right of long possession, tends to establish a valid title, may have something to do with our readier credence of old tellings; or it may be that the mere dread of the shock that always follows a discovery of falsity in whatever is hoary and venerable is sufficient account for it; but whatever the cause, we have yet to be thankful that the ancient sanctity of print is not wholly departed from ancient printings, however much in the new order it has fallen away.

Perhaps the first-printed narrative of the traditionary courtship is the matter-of-fact paragraph in the Rev. Timothy Alden's Collection of American Epitaphs and Inscriptions, which was published during the years 1812-14. In those days, on this side the Atlantic at least, ornaments of style were not encouraged, and romance, even though true, was rather frowned upon than favored by the descendants of the Puritans. Accordingly it is but the barest and most prosaic — though, you may be sure, explicit — statement of fact which suited the reverend gentleman's notion of the needs and proprieties of the theme. But here is his telling:

"It is well known that of the first company consisting of one hundred and one, about one-half died in six months after the landing in consequence of the hardships they were called to encounter. Mrs. Rose Standish, consort of Captain Standish, departed this life on the twenty-ninth of January, 1621. This circumstance is mentioned as an introduction to the following anecdote, which has been carefully handed down by tradition. In a very short time after the decease of Mrs. Standish the Captain was led to think that if he could obtain Miss Priscilla Mullins, a daughter of Mr. William Mullins, the break in his family would be happily repaired. He, therefore, according to the custom of those times, sent to ask Mr. Mullins' permission to visit his daughter. John Alden, the messenger, went and faithfully communciated the wishes of the Captain.

"The old gentleman did not object, as he might have done, on account of the recency of Captain Standish's bereavement. He said it was perfectly agreeable to him, but the young lady must also be consulted. The damsel was then called into the room, and John Alden, who is said to have been a man of most excellent form, with a fair and ruddy complexion, arose, and, in a very courteous and prepossessing manner, delivered his errand. Miss Mullins listened with respectful attention, and at last, after a considerable pause, fixing her eyes upon him, with an open and pleasant countenance, said: 'Prithee, John, why do you not speak for yourself?'

"He blushed and bowed, and took his leave, but with a look which indicated more than his diffidence would permit him otherwise to express. However, he soon renewed his visit, and it was not long before their nuptials were celebrated in ample form. From them are descended all of the name, Alden, in the United States. What report he made to his constituent, after the first interview, tradition does not unfold; but it is said, how true the writer knows not, that the Captain never forgave him to the day of his death."

It is not unlikely that it was from this version that Longfellow drew the outline of the famous idyll which has made Priscilla's romance a first adornment of the epic history of America, and Priscilla herself the best loved of American heroines. With the story of Captain John Smith and Pocahontas (which the historians, I understand, now bumptiously command us to disbelieve), the story of Captain Standish's miscarried attempt to win the maid of his choice will always remain an inseparable episode of the early romance of the land.

There is more than one odd parallel between the years apart. Each is pre-eminently the love story of the settlement where its occurrence is laid, and these settlements are the two first successful colonies of English people on the American coast. Then, too, each is distinctively a woman's story—

a heroine's story. Whatever credit there is, in either case, is the woman's; for it is not easy to see how Captain Smith or Captain Standish, John Alden, Thomas Rolfe or Powhatan, emerge with more than considerate respectability from their respective affairs. Priscilla and Pocahontas carry all the honors.

"The Courtship of Miles Standish," while inevitably the final form which the tradition is to assume, was not its first appearance in literature. Longfellow's poem was published in 1858, but as early as 1850 a version of the old story appeared in a novel entitled "A Peep at the Pilgrims in Sixteen Hundred Thirty-Six," by Mrs. H. V. Cheney, which was published in Boston. In Mrs. Cheney's novel the story is introduced merely incidentally, and not at all as a hinge to the plot.

It is much garbled, too, neither John Alden nor Priscilla being parties to it, while Captain Standish is only accidentally the butt of the tale. But it is of interest as a form of the tradition, and not a little also for the type of heroine which Mrs. Cheney conceives necessary to the theme — a heroine whose lack of maidenly modesty and unquestionable tendency toward slang are all at variance with our orthodox picture of a Puritan Priscilla. It is in a letter given as written by Peregrine White, whom the author paints almost pertinaciously vivacious, that the incident is narrated:

"Did Miriam tell you — though it is not likely she did — that Mr. Calvert left Plymouth soon after you went away, and everybody says because she would not marry him and go to Virginia. Well, as his vessel was not quite ready to sail, he went to pass a week or two with Captain Standish, who it seems took a great liking to him. It so happened that while he was there the captain saw by chance a comely young damsel, and thinking, as well he might, that it was not good for a man to be alone, he resolved in his mind the means of taking her unto himself for wife. But as it is long since his courting days, I suppose the good man felt a little awkward at the business, being more accustomed to slashing up Indians than making fine speeches, such as win pretty women; and so in imitation of ancient Isaac he resolved to send forward a herald to speak the word for him.

"I have ever since thought he would have done well if he had chosen me, who would, doubtless, have proven a trusty agent, but instead thereof he selected Calvert, who was at his house, and well able to argue fluently on any side of the question, right or wrong. So he repaired to the damsel, full armed with instructions; but, alas! who can foresee the caprices of love? When he had finished pleading the captain's cause, the maiden turned her bewitching eyes upon him, and said with sweet simplicity:

'Prithee, why do you not speak for yourself?'

'Would you,' answered Calvert, 'prefer me, an unknown stranger, to the brave captain whose name is renowned all over the world for his deeds of courage?'

'Ten to one,' replied the damsel, with a smile and a blush.

"Now the rest of their conference is unknown, and this has leaked out unawares, but it was doubtless settled to the satisfaction of both, for Calvert returned to Captain Standish to confess the strange result of the business, and arrange his affairs; and it is whispered that your valiant kinsman flew into a most violent passion, and that very night turned him out of doors. I will not vouch for the truth of all this, being very cautious about spreading reports, — but be that as it may, before noon on the following day, Mr. Calvert put his bride and other commodities on board the vessel, and sailed from Plymouth, probably forever."

If Mrs. Cheney's narrative is the first, it is yet not the last novelist's attempt to deal with the story. In Jane G. Austin's artful little novel, "Standish of Standish," the tale appears once again, and in rather a more vital connection to its setting. The version in "Standish of Standish" is a palpably labored attempt on the part of the authoress to save the good captain, who is the hero of her novel, from what is at best a mirth-provoking situation. And in order to do this she mangles it with a hand so insensitive to the qualities that go to make up a good story that it is hard to forgive the maladroitness, even for the sake of anotherwise charming tale.

It is to be doubted, too, if in treating him thus the authoress is not doing an unkindness to the brave captain; for it is difficult to credit him with a lack of the good graces of humor or a hardness of heart so great that he would not willingly play the sorrier part for the sake of the tale and its perpetuity. And, indeed, history (not of the sour sort), seems to record a certain jolly acquiescence on his part to the featherings of fate, for not only was he a life-long friend and neighbor of Master Alden and his household, but, as if to set fitting seal and climax to the romance of the courtship, he sanctioned his son's union with Priscilla's daughter,—a final touch which no wonder-tale could have bettered.

But in Mrs. Austin's novel the captain is made a victim of neighborly gossip, of woman's wile and of a soldierly sense of honor. Desire Minter is at the bottom of the affair and the scapegoat for all blame and blunder. She it is, who, desirous of wedding the newly-widowed Captain Standish, and madly jealous of Priscilla whom she deems an aspirant, not unfavored, in the same direction, spreads abroad the report that the two are betrothed or like to be.

The impression arising from this report, interpreted by the Colony as an expectation on Priscilla's part, is supplemented by a promise given by the captain to Mr. Mullins on his death-bed that he would keep ward over his family — a promise which is construed by Governor Bradford as a pledge of marriage, so understood by both Priscilla and her father. Thus brought home to the Captain, it becomes a matter of soldierly honor to fulfill the pledge, even though he himself had been under no such impression, and had no desire to wed Priscilla.

So he delegates John Alden — who is represented with only a modicum of brains to savor a plenum of muscle, but with a dog-like faithfulness of heart — to inform the maiden that he is graciously willing to stand by the bargain into which he finds himself inadvertently drawn, — a proposal which she, all unsuspicious, not unnaturally resents.

But the true humor of the situation (for the reader, that is; since it must be confessed that the authoress woefully wants this saving salt) appears in the introduction of Priscilla's oft-quoted phrase. John Alden is represented as a long-suffering, oft-suing and oft-spurned wooer of the maid whom he eventually wins by the brute force of pertinacity. In his poor blundering way he has made it as clear as may be to Priscilla herself and to the sympathetic onlookers (Captain Standish being the one obtuse member of the Colony) what is the desire of his heart. And in the climactic scene he is goaded by the maid's taunts to the ninth declaration of his love. It is in the midst of this declaration, just as he is desperately averring that he loves her "as blind men love sight, and dying men water," — speaking for himself if ever man so spoke, and consciencelessly flinging his mission to the winds, — that Priscilla cuts him short with:

"Then why don't you speak for yourself, John?" Could anything be more mercilessly malapropos?

It is safe to say that "Standish of Standish" luckily fails in its thankless endeavor to spoil a good story, and because the failure is so thorough-going and sincere we may forgive the authoress her attempt and preserve her volume for its better qualities. One need only compare this tale with the earlier "Peep" of Mrs. Cheney's to perceive what these qualities are, and to thank the pains which has given us a chatty acquaintanceship with the Pilgrim Fathers, and more of a human hold on them than the historians would allow.

A better interpretation (and this can truly be called an interpretation, and not a version) is Harriet Prescott Spofford's "Priscilla" in the "Three Heroines of New England Romance," published only a half dozen years ago. Mrs. Spofford takes Priscilla and John Alden as sensitive, high-spirited, and delicately minded, yet serious and ardent lovers, just as Longfellow portrays them; and upon the incidents and scenes which made their story theirs before it became ours, she touches with the gentle hand and quick sympathy of one who feels and understands all that must have happened. It is for Priscilla's sake that her sketch is written, and if you wish to know Priscilla more intimately than even Longfellow's poem portrays her, if you wish to know Priscilla as a woman, and as a woman sees her, you cannot do better than to know her through Mrs. Spofford's sketch. It is not a story of incidents that she gives us, but the fine-spun web of a love's psychology; and here it cannot in any way be recast. It must be sought out for its own sake, between the covers of its native book.

But the story that is to stand and the version of it that is always to remain the orthodox version is the poet's. And if John Alden was in reality not at all the scholar whom Longfellow describes, and if Captain Standish may have been of a less epic prowess and Priscilla possibly of a more Gallic temperament, still the soul of the story is none the less truly incarnate in the poem and the portraits themselves are truest in being true to that soul. For us Captain Standish will ever remain the "rough old soldier, grown grim and gray in the harness," while John Alden will always appear the white-faced lover, torn between the conflicting demands of leal friendship and his heart's need, who, bearing the gift of dewy Mayflowers, bursts with trembling eloquence upon the frighted Priscilla. And she — can Priscilla herself ever be anything other than the "loveliest maiden of Plymouth," in whose garb, redolent of romance, the maids of today best love to masquerade, whose form and feature it is so often the delight of our artists to portray?

"Seated beside her wheel, and the carded wool
like a snow-drift
Piled at her knee, her white hand feeding the
ravenous spindle,
While with her foot on the treadle she guided the
wheel in its motion."

PABODIE HOUSE, LITTLE COMPTON, R. I.

CHAPTER X.

A PILGRIM HOUSEHOLD.

IT is probable that John and Priscilla were married late in 1621 or early the following year. Their first child may have been born in 1622, which is the date Ebenezer Alden in his "Memorial of the Descendants of the Hon. John Alden" sets for the birth of Captain John Alden, later of Boston, — but it is more probable that 1624 was the year which saw the first addition to the newly established household, for it was in this year that Elizabeth Alden, afterward Paybodie, gladdened the eyes of her young parents. Between that date and the allotment of cattle in 1627, when we know that there were four members of the Alden family, John, the eldest son, was born. These two and Joseph, the second son, born in 1627, were doubtless all born in Plymouth, under the shadow of old Fort Hill, but the remaining children must have been natives of Duxbury.

We know from Governor Bradford's entry of 1651 that at that time John and Priscilla were the parents of eleven children, but the names of certain of these children are largely a matter of conjecture. The attestation of settlement of John Alden's estate, signed by his heirs, (quoted on page 100) is the most complete list which we possess, but even here there are no more than ten names and several of these are signatures of the sons-in-law and possibly in one case of a daughter-in-law of the Pilgrim.

Mrs. Charles L. Alden, in her Alden Genealogy, has presented a list of the children of John and Priscilla, together with the dates of their births, and while her work may be modified by future discoveries, it is undoubtedly in the main correct. She gives the names and dates as follows:

Elizabeth, born 1623-4.
John, born 1626.
Joseph, born 1627.
Sarah, born 1629.
Jonathan, born 1632-3.
Ruth, born 1634-5.
Rebecca, born about 1637.
Priscilla.
Zachariah, born perhaps about 1641.
Mary, born perhaps about 1643.
David, born 1646.

The names in this list that are represented in the

certificate of settlement are: Elizabeth, by her husband, William Paybody; Mary, by her husband, Thomas Delano; Sarah and Ruth, who were both dead in 1688, are represented by their husbands' signatures; Priscilla, presumably an unmarried daughter, but concerning her nothing is known beyond this signature; Rebecca was probably dead at this time, and without children, for which reason she is unrepresented. Of the sons, John, Joseph and David sign for themselves; Jonathan, of course, is named in the certification; and it is presumed that the signature of Mary Alden is as the wife of Zachariah, who was probably absent, or possibly dead, at the time.

This list in every way satisfies Governor Bradford's entry and appears to be an altogether probable restoration of the family, although there is necessarily some doubt in connection with the names of Zachariah, Rebecca and Priscilla. It is not absolutely sure that the Mary who signed the attestation of settlement was the wife of Zachariah, nor is it impossible that the Priscilla whose name appears there was not the Pilgrim's wife, as Ebenezer Alden not unnaturally supposed. Nevertheless the reasons given by the author of the Alden

Genealogy for her interpretation are sufficiently convincing.

It is known that Mary, the daughter of John and Priscilla, was married to Thomas Delano, who signs in her right. Her name at that time must have been Mary Delano, and the "Mary Alden" whose name appears could not, therefore, have been she, but was most likely, as Mrs. Alden surmises, the wife of another son — the Zachariah of whom some trace exists. As for Priscilla — it is almost certain that Priscilla, the mother, died before this time. At all events, there has been discovered no later mention of her.

Concerning the eight other children there is, of course, no doubt, and it is through them that all descent from the Pilgrim John is traced.

Elizabeth was the eldest of these. She was born in Plymouth in 1623 or '24,— the first white woman native to New England soil. On December twenty-six, 1644, she was married to William Pabodie. This wedding took place in Duxbury, where she then lived, and was doubtless performed by her father, already long a magistrate. It was not until forty years later, in 1684, that the Pabodies removed to Little Compton, R. I., where their final home was made. Their residence while in Dux-

THE ATTIC CHIMNEY

bury was "east of Eagle Nest Creek, and near Brewster and Standish."

Here were born their thirteen children,—John, Elizabeth, Mary, Mercy, Martha, Priscilla (dying in early infancy), Priscilla, Sarah, Ruth, Rebecca, Hannah, William and Lydia,—and here ten of them were married. It was here, too, in 1669, that John, the eldest son, was killed by a blow from the bough of a tree, sustained while riding beneath it.

William Pabodie, the husband, was a man of some moment both in Duxbury and Little Compton. He was possessed of considerable property, and for many years held public office. He lived to the ripe old age of eighty-seven, having been born in 1620 and dying in 1707.

But in years the husband did not equal the wife. Mrs. Pabodie lived until 1717 and it was in the "Boston News Letter" of the seventeenth of June in that year that the following notice appeared:

"Little Compton, May thirty-one, 1717. This morning died here Mrs. Elizabeth Paybody, in the ninety-third year of her age. She was a daughter of John Alden, Esquire, and Priscilla, his wife, daughter of Mr. William Mullens. This John Alden and Priscilla Mullens were married at Plymouth, where their daughter Elizabeth was born. She was exemplary, virtuous and pious, and her memory is blessed. She left a numerous posterity. Her granddaughter Bradford is a grandmother."

It is in connection with the last sentence of this brief biography that an ancient couplet is handed down as referring to Elizabeth Pabodie, who, in her great-great-grandmother's capacity, loquitur:

"Rise, daughter, to thy daughter run!
Thy daughter's daughter hath a son!"

The Aldens as a family have ever been long-lived and fruitful of posterity, and in more than one modern instance four generations are co-existent, but it is doubtful if there has ever been another case where members of five generations were living at the one time.

Elizabeth Pabodie was buried in Little Compton and there may still be seen a granite shaft in the old burying-ground bearing the inscription: "Here lyeth the body of Elizabeth Pabodie, who dyed May ye thirty-first, 1717, and in the ninety-fourth year of her age."

The Pabodie house, built in 1680, is still well preserved, and is now inhabited by Mr. George Gray and his family. Mrs. Gray is descended from Innocent Howland, known to tradition as "the beautiful Quakeress." During repairs, some years

Elizabeth Pabodie Monument, Little Compton.
Original Gravestone and Inscription.

since, curious relics were discovered in ancient ashes under the hearth, among them a bronze spoon of a fashion used in Holland at the time of the Pilgrimage. This spoon has passed into the possession of a descendant of Elizabeth Pabodie.

The most picturesque career of any of the children of the Pilgrim was that of Captain John Alden of Boston. Born in Plymouth about 1626, he passed his earlier years in Duxbury where the records show that he was admitted freeman in 1646. Three years later he removed to Boston, which was thenceforth to be his home, his dwelling being situated on a passage leading from Cambridge Street to Sudbury Street, and called after him "Alden's Lane,"—today known as Alden Street.

In his youth he became a mariner and in later years rose to eminence in his profession and acquired by means of it what was in his day something of a fortune. He was for some years master of a merchantman owned by John Hull, and later for many years commander of the armed vessel belonging to the Colony of Massachusetts Bay which supplied the Maine posts with provisions and stores. He also saw service in the French and Indian wars, and in 1691 a vessel in his charge was taken by a French frigate, and he and his son were made prisoners,—not, however, for a long captivity. But by far the most interesting episode in Captain Alden's career was his arrest and trial as a witch, and as of all those so accused he is the only one who has left us a written account of his experiences, his case is of exceptional interest. The narrative is given in Upham's "History of Witchcraft," as follows:

"John Alden, Sr., of Boston, in the county of Suffolk, mariner, on the twenty-eighth day of May, 1692, was sent for by the magistrates of Salem, in the county of Essex, upon the accusation of a company of poor distracted or possessed creatures or witches; and being sent by Mr. Stoughton, arrived there on the thirty-first of May, and appeared at Salem Village, before Mr. Gedney, Mr. Hawthorne and Mr. Corwin.

"Those wenches being present who played their juggling tricks, falling down, crying out, and staring in people's faces, the magistrates demanded of them several times who it was of all the people in the room that hurt them. One of these accusers pointed several times at one Captain Hill, there present, but spake nothing. The same accuser had a man standing at her back to hold her up. He stooped down to her ear; then she cried out, 'Alden, Alden afflicted her.' One of the magistrates asked her if she had ever seen Alden. She answered 'No.' He asked her how she knew it was Alden. She said the man told her so.

"Then all were ordered to go down in the street, where a ring was made; and the same accuser cried out, 'There stands Alden, a bold fellow, with his hat on before the judges; he sells powder and shot to the Indians and French. . . . ' Then was Alden committed to the marshal's custody, and his sword taken from him; for they said he afflicted them with his sword. After some hours Alden was sent for to the meeting-house in the village, before the magistrates, who required Alden to stand upon a chair, to the open view of all the people.

"The accusers cried out that Alden pinched them then, when he stood upon the chair, in the sight of all the people, a good way distant from them. One of the magistrates bid the marshal to hold open Alden's hands, that he might not pinch those creatures. , Alden asked them why they should think that he should come to that village to afflict those persons that he never knew or saw before. Mr. Gedney bid Alden confess and give glory to God.

"Alden said he hoped he should give glory to

God and hoped he should never gratify the devil: but appealed to all that ever knew him, if they ever suspected him to be such a person; and challenged any one that could bring in anything on their own knowledge, that might give suspicion of his being such an one. Mr. Gedney said he had known Alden many years, and had been at sea with him, and always looked upon him to be an honest man; but now he saw cause to alter his judgment. Alden answered, he was sorry for that, but he hoped God would clear up his innocency, that he would recall that judgment again; and added that he hoped that he should, with Job, maintain his integrity till he died.

"They bid Alden look upon his accusers, which he did, and then they fell down. Alden asked Mr. Gedney what reason there could be given why Alden's looking upon him did not strike him down as well, but no reason was given that I heard. But the accusers were brought to Alden to touch them; and this touch, they said, made them well. Alden began to speak of the Providence of God in suffering these creatures to accuse innocent persons.

"Mr. Noyes asked Alden why he should offer to speak of the Providence of God: God, by his Providence (said Mr. Noyes), governs the world, and keeps it in peace; and so went on with discourse, and stopped Alden's mouth as to that. Alden told Gedney that he could assure him that there was a lying spirit in them; for I can assure you that there is not a word of truth in all these say of me. But Alden was again committed to the marshal, and his mittimus written.

"To Boston Alden was carried by a constable: no bail would be taken for him, but was delivered to the prison-keeper, where he remained fifteen weeks; and then, observing the manner of trials, and evidence then taken, was at length prevailed with to make his escape."

From the prison Captain Alden made his way to Duxbury, where he aroused his relatives in the middle of the night with the information that "he was flying from the devil and the devil was after him." He remained there for several months, until the witchery scare had subsided, when he gave himself up to the authorities at Boston and no one appearing against him, he was discharged,—but with a temper forever after soured against any mention of witchcraft.

Captain Alden was married twice, each time to an Elizabeth. The first wife died before 1660, for this was the year in which he married Elizabeth

Everill, widow, who remained to share his home until 1695 or '96. He himself lived until 1702, when he died at the age of seventy-five. According to Ebenezer Alden's Memorial he was the father of fourteen children, at least four of whom died in early infancy. At the present day there are no descendants of Captain Alden bearing the name.

When he first came to Boston Captain Alden united by letter with the "First Church" of that city, but later joined the secession from that church which resulted in the organization of the "Third Church," afterward the Old South Church, of which he was thus a charter member. Today his gravestone is one of three preserved under the portico of the New Old South Church building at the corner of Copley Square in that city. The story of its recovery is given in the Boston Transcript for April thirty, 1870, as follows:

"Mr. Samuel Jennison, the owner of property on and about Carlton Place, has recently, on account of the widening ot Eliot Street, begun operations for the purpose of building there a new block. As the excavations have been going on some relics of the past have been dug up, including a lot of bones and quite a number of gravestones, some of them nearly whole. These are small slate

TABLET IN THE NEW OLD SOUTH CHURCH, BOSTON.

stone tablets, such as may be seen in the King's Chapel, Granary, and other ancient burying-grounds in the vicinity, and most of them have the old-fashioned death's head cut over their inscriptions."

The inscription upon Captain Alden's stone reads, "Here lyeth the body of John Alden, Senior, aged seventy-five years. Deceased March fourteen, 1702." The stone was consecrated, in its present position, in 1884, Hamilton A. Hill delivering upon that occasion a memorial address.

Concerning the second son, Joseph, we know nothing beyond the bare skeleton of dates which is too often the sum of the life notes which the forefathers have left to us. Joseph Alden was a farmer in Bridgewater, where he held lands deeded to him by his father; and doubtless he fulfilled well the duties of his station and lived well the traditions of his parentage — a son worthy the parents. Certainly his neighbors thought well of him, for he held local offices in his town and served the Colony on the "Grand Inquest."

And if a man's posterity may speak for the man, as surely it ought, Joseph Alden was not one who neglected the religious duties and privileges of the Pilgrim Church; at all events we find among his descendants an unusually long and persistent succession of ministers of the Gospel.

He was named "Joseph" after Priscilla's younger brother, who was among the victims of that fatal first winter of 1620-21, and there is a tradition in certain branches of the family that he was Priscilla's favorite among all her children.

Joseph Alden was born, in Plymouth, about the year 1627, and certainly after the cattle division of that year, since in the record of the division John Alden's family comprises only the two older children. But as this was in May, it is not unlikely that Joseph was born later in the same year. The date given by Ebenezer Alden, 1624, is certainly incorrect.

Joseph Alden was married in 1659, presumably in Duxbury, where he may have resided some years, since he did not receive the Bridgewater lands until 1679, although to be sure this was not the date of his removal thither. His wife was Mary, daughter of Moses Simmons. To them were born five, or possibly seven, children. Ebenezer Alden gives: Isaac, Joseph, John, Elizabeth, and Mary; and to this list Mrs. Chas. Alden adds a probable Mercy and Elizabeth. Joseph Alden died

February eighth, 1697, leaving an estate valued at seventy-six pounds.

Sarah, the second daughter of John and Priscilla, was born, according to Mrs. Alden, about the time of the removal to Duxbury. She it was who, by her marriage with Alexander Standish, son of the captain, played the graceful last scene in the comedy of the courtship; and if there ever was more than the good-humored banter of neighbors in the old story of the stout captain's long-nursed wrath — a story hard to credit,— we cannot doubt that to Sarah, his rival's daughter but his heir's bride, must belong the honor of having at length conquered the sad distemper; and no doubt, too, she delivered the coup de grace with a smack of her rosy lips, nor can we believe that the captain's animosity fell an unwilling victim.

The fruit of this match was a family of seven — Lorah, Lydia, Mercy, Elizabeth, Sarah, Miles and Ebenezer. They dwelt in a house still standing, built by Alexander Standish, not far from the Alden estate. Sarah, the wife, died in her early maturity, and her husband married again, but no children were born of the second marriage. Alexander Standish participated in the public life of the community, serving as deputy from Duxbury, and for a number of years as town clerk. He died in 1702.

Captain Jonathan Alden of Duxbury was the Pilgrim's third son. He was born about 1632 and may have been the first of the children born in Duxbury. As he grew up he showed that inclination for military affairs which has always been characteristic of the family. He was successively an ensign, lieutenant and captain in the Duxbury contingent of the Colony's force, and his military service was of many years duration. When he died, in 1697, he was buried under arms, the Rev. Mr. Wiswall at the time delivering an address at his grave, portions of which are still handed down to us, being preserved in Timothy Alden's collection of epitaphs and inscriptions.

Captain Jonathan inherited the paternal homestead in Duxbury and it was probably with him that the Pilgrim parents spent their last days. He was administrator of his father's estate, as we have seen. He did not marry until late in life, unless there was an earlier marriage than the one recorded with Abigail Hallett in 1672. He was the father of five or six children, presumably all by this wife. Of his burial place Mrs. Chas. Alden writes: "He and his wife are buried in the cemetery in South Duxbury, half a mile from the railroad station. His stone was broken away from its place, and Miss Lucia Alden Bradford — a descendant — took it to her home and kept it framed in her parlor. Before her death, a few years since, she sent me a copy of the stone. It has since been reset near the grave of his wife. It reads: 'Here lyes ye body of Jonathan Alden. Died February ye fourteen, 1697, in ye sixty-fifth year of his age.'"

In regard to the Zachariah, which the author of the Alden Genealogy includes in the family, we may best quote her own words:

"We have less knowledge of Zachariah than of any of the sons. He undoubtedly married a wife Mary, who, in the settlement of John Alden's estate, signed with the rest of the heirs for her husband — he being absent or dead. I think he was absent, for the marriage notice of their daughter Anna to Josiah Snell reads: 'Josiah Snell of Bridgewater to Anna Alden, daughter of Zachariah Alden of Duxbury.' Josiah and Anna (Alden) Snell were ancestors of the poet Bryant. Among their descendants I find two traditions: one that Zachariah was a minister or teacher; the other that he was a mariner. I think the latter is more probable, for I do not find him on the Duxbury lists. The name Zachariah appears in his brother John's family. We have also a tradition that Anna (Alden) Snell had a brother Zachariah and I think it probable that the Mary Alden who married Samuel Allen in 1700 was his daughter, who was in Bridgewater visiting her sister.

"On the list of freemen, May twenty-ninth, 1670, in Duxbury, is a John Alden, Jr. At that time Capt. John Alden was in Boston, and it looks to me as if there were a son of Zachariah who might be old enough to serve. At any rate I place this John in Zachariah's family. I know nothing further of him.

"There is no will or settlement of the estate, and altogether this family is very unsatisfactory. We know John Alden had eleven children. We have found ten — and the strong family tradition in the poet Bryant's family — the name Zachariah in Captain John's family — the Mary, wife of some son, who signs the receipt of heirs — all lead us to place Zachariah as the missing child."

Of the two remaining daughters concerning whom we know more than the mere name, Ruth, the elder, ancestress of the Presidents Adams, was born some time during the years 1634-6. On the "12 mo. 3 d. 1657, John Bass and Ruth Aulden were married by Mr. John Aulden of Duxbury," as the old record tells us. Seven children were born of this wedding: John, Samuel, Ruth, Joseph, Hannah, Mary, Sarah. The mother died in 1674 at her home in Braintree, but John Bass lived to marry a second time and for many a year thereafter, dying in 1716.

Mary, the youngest daughter of John and Priscilla, was born in 1643. In 1667 she married Dr. Thomas Delano, son of the Huguenot Pilgrim, Philip de la Noye, who came to Plymouth in the "Fortune" in 1621. The date of Mary Delano's death is not known. Eight children are attributed to her: Benoni, Thomas, Jonathan, David, Mary, Sarah, Ruth and Joseph.

The youngest child of the Pilgrim was the son David. He was born in Duxbury in 1646. In 1670 he married Mercy, daughter of Constant Southworth, the latter a son by her first husband, Edward Southworth, of Governor Bradford's second wife, Alice. He died in 1719. He owned land in Duxbury, Pembroke and Middleborough, part of it at least deeded to him by his father. His children were: Henry, Ruth, Elizabeth, Priscilla, Benjamin, Alice and Samuel.

Concerning David Alden, Justin Winsor says that he "was much employed in the public business of the town, one of its selectmen, its deputy and likewise an assistant in the government. He was a prominent member of the church, said to have been one of its deacons, and a man of the highest respectability."

Thus briefly is finished the count of the household of John and Priscilla Alden. Concerning most of the children our information is very meagre, but we know enough to be well assured that the family was one that honored the parents which gave so many useful citizens to the community, and we cannot but believe that in their older years these parents were well rejoiced in their offspring. While none of the sons left a reputation equal to the father's and none of the daughters a romance such as the mother's, still each occupied a position of usefulness and trust in the growing community so that the family as a whole contributed not a little to its substantial development. They were loyal sons of the state and devout daughters of the church, these sons and daughters of Pilgrim Alden, and they performed well the duties which were theirs.

It is notable that no son of John Alden shows quite the versatile range of activity of the father. Not one of them but had varied interests, yet each shows a narrowing bent, carrying on one or two branches of the parent's work, leaving the remainder to the other brothers, so that in the whole family of sons we find nearly all of John Alden's employments represented.

Thus Captain John was a mariner and soldier, Captain Jonathan a soldier and farmer, Joseph a farmer, David farmer, deputy and deacon. This was natural enough, for it betokened the beginnings of that process of specialization even yet going on in our midst. The infant Colony was out of its swaddling clothes; it was assuming the form and organization of a state; the foundations, laid at the framing of the Pilgrim Compact, were tested and found firm, and the superstructure of a great civilization was being reared upon it. And the part which they and their descendants have played in this rearing is not a little to the credit and glory of the vigorous Alden stock firm planted in the New Land.

CHAPTER XI.

THE OLD HOME AT DUXBURY.

NTERING Duxbury from Plymouth via the Old Colony Railroad, you may notice, just as the train is slowing down for its stop at Duxbury station, on the right and not far from the road-bed, an old-time house of the type most common in this eldest neighborhood of New England. There is the great central chimney, with the house seemingly built around it; there are the plain, rectangular lines of Puritan architecture; there are the unpainted walls, covered with shingles rather than clapboard; the small windows with many panes,—all the weather-brunting characteristics of the early Cape Cod builder.

At a glance you will recognize the house as one of the first made, and if you are of the lineage of Alden, come thither for the first time, the recognition may be of a more intimate sort and accompanied by a thrill of something like a long-looked-for home-return. For this old house is the home-

VIEW OF DUXBURY.

stead of the Aldens, the nursery, they tell us, of the children of John and Priscilla.

Every recurring summer season counts scores of pilgrims, descendants of that Pilgrim of other days, bound for this Mecca of their race; and every recurring autumn finds as fruit of this in the pilgrims' many homes a renewed and invigorated patriotism and honest family pride. For the old house is in a way the symbol of the splendid vitality of those in whose veins the blood of John Alden is perpetuated. It is now almost two hundred and fifty years that it has sheltered, as still it shelters, children and childrens' children of the family's founder.

No other American family can show such a record of local stability; and while there are a few older houses in New England, there is none which has been held so long in the family of the original builder. It is to be hoped that the record may be continued unbroken, and that while the house is preserved it may remain in the hands of its builder's kindred.

John Alden's farmstead in Duxbury originally contained about one hundred and sixty-nine acres. The land is low and slightly rolling, well watered and fertile. It has long been considered one of the best portions of farming land in the town. Nowadays most of the original land has been alienated from the family and only the house with the few acres of land forming the house lot remain in Alden possession. But many of the ancient landmarks are still preserved.

There is the little knoll upon which John Alden's first Duxbury home was reared,—in 1627, the weather-worn slab, there erected, tells us. To the south of this knoll is meadowland leading down to the wooded shores of Eagle Tree Pond — a beautiful little lake, in summer fringed with rushes and water lilies, its tree-clad borders eloquent with the bird-poetry native to New England woodland. Most interesting of all are the ancient Eagle Trees from which the pond derived its name. These two trees stand solitary in the midst of swamp fields, their strained and twisted branches, once the favorite perches of the now-vanished eagles, mutely attesting their long-endured struggle with wind and frost.

The landscape is characteristic of the vicinity. On every side are fields and lowlands, alternating meadow and garden, house lot and wood lot. Occasionally, rising abruptly from the lower level, a hill or group of hills such as the tall land-rise to the east which protects the homestead on the seaward side. Of course there are houses — of many types and generations, from the strong-founded dwellings of the first comers to the snugly comfortable modern cottage.

And close at hand is the railway,— the bell and whistle of the locomotive summoning back into the present, with sharp command, the errant fancy which would seek too freely on this ground of memories the vanished realities of the past.

But despite the proximity of blatant modernity (for surely a steam engine is nothing less), one cannot stand before the old house, noting its bending beams, its creased and furrowed surfaces,— for an old house, like an old man, becomes bowed and wrinkled,— without feeling somewhat the venerable mystery of age. The old scenes, the old inhabitants,— you almost expect to see a tall Pilgrim step from the door, buckled and breeched and leathered, with bell-mouthed blunderbuss or flintlock and rest at his shoulder, as the old prints have taught us to picture him. Or it may be that you look for the demure Puritan maiden, none the less charming for all her gray garb, and adept, as maids are bound to be somehow or other, with kerchief coquetry. And then the ear, eager to supplement the mind's eye's vision, wakes to a musical humming that can be nothing other than the song of the spinning-wheel, from which momentarily, as from the opening chords of the orchestra, you expect to hear the voice of the singer catch up the thread of melody and weave it into the more intimate music of the heart's desire.

Probably your revery — if so you lose yourself — will very soon be broken by some one of the ever-recurring reminders of modern life — the whistle or the clang of cars, the petulant puffing of the swift-passing automobile, or yet the energetic speech of the acclimated American, far different from the gentle "prithee" and the archaic "thou" and "thine" of our forefathers. So awakening, with Twentieth century earth underfoot, the bright sun shedding daylight all about, you lock your fancy tight in its dark closet and enter the old house with firm resolve to see only with modern eyes.

Now, ten to one, the fancy will steal out upon you unawares before ever you have set foot across the threshold. The lure is too strong and your lock too insecure. But is it not better so? If you would know it at its best, the old place must be seen with all the eyes God has given you, and the eye of the imagination is not the dullest among these. Neither must you close your ears, for there are whisperings of the ancient rafters which only the ear tuned to sympathy with their tales may hope to hear. Then, fancy free, let us enter.

At first step — if we go in by the front door which faces south — we find ourselves in a little hallway with doors to the right and to the left and before us, creeping up the broad central buttress of chimney, a narrow wooden stairway, almost ladder-like in its steepness. We stop, perhaps, to note the old woodwork with marks of the original tooling, crude but hearty, still plain, and those other scars due to the wear and accident of time. How many, many feet have trodden these stairs,— beginning, it may be, as creeping children to whom the surmounting of each separate step is new achievement; ending as the trembling octogenarian who steadies his slow descent by careful grasp of the rude hand-rail. A stairway is somehow always symbolic of the risings and settings of the lives of those who pass up and down.

But we do not follow the stair now. We turn rather to the door at the right and enter the Great Room, as our fathers called the apartment wherein was centered the social dignities of their home life. This room is about seventeen by twenty feet in its horizontal dimensions and about nine feet high. There are windows — each with its twelve small panes — on both the southern and eastern sides of the room.

In addition to the door leading from the hallway, there is another on the opposite side of the chimney opening into the living room. Originally nearly the whole western side of the Great Room was occupied by a capacious fireplace hollowed out on this side of the big chimney, but later most of the space was covered with a paneling of wood, and a small iron grate, about sixty years old, is the modern means of heating. In this room are gathered the few relics of the early dwellers that still remain in the house — plates and platters of old pewter, one or two antique chairs, bits of hand-wrought iron. There is also here to be seen a large picture representing John Alden in his courtship days holding the yarn which Priscilla, with pretty tyranny, winds for her spinning. This picture, they tell us, was designed by Mr. John Tolman Alden of St. Louis, and executed at his order.

In one corner of the room is a built-in cupboard, and here, we may imagine, the Pilgrim Father must have kept his choicer treasures, his books, and among them that well-thumbed Bible which lies under the glass in Pilgrim Hall at Plymouth. Doubtless it was in this room that the family prayers were held, and so we think of John and Priscilla in their maturer years, with children and grandchildren gathered about them, leading the simple devotions of morning and evening after the custom of those of the Congregation of Leyden. Later, perhaps, when the son Jonathan had succeeded to the headship of the family, and old eyes were less ready in following even familiar texts, they must still have gathered as before, except that now the grandsire held son's son on his knee while the two listened to the deep-voiced reading of him who had succeeded to the duties and responsibilities of active family leadership.

Near this corner cupboard or closet is a panel of wood behind which, being raised, you may see the date of the erection of the house, "1653," cut into the planking. It was a goodly custom of the early builder and has preserved to us the date of building of the Munroe Tavern at Lexington and other old structures of historic interest.

Passing from the Great Room, we enter the Living Room. This was in olden times pre-eminently the woman's domain, and consequently here centered all the livelier domestic activities. It is a long, narrow room, less than a dozen feet wide and in length fully three-fourths of the longer dimension of the house, and that is forty feet or more. At the eastern side of it is an entry-way and door; at the western a small bed-room. On the northern side are windows and doorway leading into the annex added in later years to the original house.

Opposite is a broadside of the great chimney—twelve or fifteen feet square at the base,—and here formerly was another huge fireplace, the most important in the house, since it was the hearth of the cookery. We cannot think of those early New England dinners, especially when the great Thanksgiving feast came round, without a certain appetitive wistfulness for the good things of other days. We wonder, too, how far the delicacies which we are accustomed to associate with that season of cheer were known to its mistress when the big fireplace cooked its first Thanksgiving dinner. The turkey certainly,—but the Indian pudding, the brown bread, the chowders, the pumpkin and above all the toothsome mince pie—all these higher achievements of New England cookery.

Doubtless Priscilla played her part in the development of these dainties, and it would be vastly interesting to her descendants to know just what that part was. The housewife in those days was thrown much upon her own resources and inventiveness — for which may posterity ever be grateful! — and the creations of her handicraft reflect no small credit on the vigor of her abilities. Something may have been borrowed from the Indians — raw materials — but the culinary achievement was hers.

In the early days the Living Room served not only as kitchen and dining room, but also as nursery, sewing and spinning room, and as gathering hall for family life and neighborly gossip. Here in preference to the more austere Great Room the young folks spent their winter evenings with games and merry-making, apples and chestnuts and cider, while oftener than not, we may imagine, the elders chose this genial setting for their own graver converse.

From the Living Room we take a peep into the little bed-room at the western end where, tradition has it, both John and Priscilla breathed their final mortal breath. It is a tiny chamber, but it opened into the warmest and cheeriest of the home apartments and so was most suitable for those subject to the chills of approaching age.

We enter now the parlor, or Best Room, as our

forefathers' more simply picturesque language termed it. It is parallel with the Great Room and of about the same size. This room was doubtless reserved for the reception of functionaries, Governor Bradford, the elders, ministers and guests who came hither on business or to take counsel with Magistrate Alden. Doubtless, too, this was the room alloted the maids for the reception of young men who came a-wooing. After the marriage, though, we can imagine that the young folks were glad to go back to the Living Room, on their home returns, and to the family society there gathered. Which was right enough and as it ought to be, for courting is at best a selfishness of two — necessary, no doubt, but happiest when gotten safely over.

Leaving the Best Room, we re-enter the hallway, and now we climb that curious narrow stairway up over the broad shoulder of the chimney. We turn again to the right and enter the Guest Room which is just above the Great Room. The first thing to attract our attention is the odd three-panelled door whereby we enter. We see the characteristics of hand workmanship and when we learn that the door is reputed to have been taken from the earlier house on the Duxbury farm, we can but wonder

THE STAIR, ALDEN HOUSE.

if the door may not have been the work of John Alden himself, for we know that first of all he was an adept toolsman. The low ceiling, the curious built-in dresser, the great axe-hewn beams of support in the corners, which in this upper story are bare to the eye, are other points of interest. We cannot but regret, here as elsewhere in the house, the necessity for paint and paper that conceal with immodest modesty the naked strength of the primitive structure. It is so in all the five remaining sleeping rooms which occupy this floor. Only in the queer little windows, the rough corner beams, the doors and casings is the old builders' craft apparent.

There is, however, a little glimpse of it in the divided door that leads into the attic of the annex—a door of the sort we sometimes see pictured, the lower half of which kept truant-tending babes within, while the upper half, swung open, served in fair weather as an extra window and sun-vent. Of course that could not have been a use of a door placed as this one, and we must guess that it was brought hither after having done service elsewhere.

Another odd door, with two little diamond-shaped windows in it, leads up to the great attic of the original house, where, better than in any other place, the ribs and beams of the house may be observed. It is a dark old attic, in the centre the big plastered chimney sloping up to the roof, overhead bare rafters, and all about enough musty gloom to give it the congenial savor of antiquity. We examine a loosened brick, probably an early importation from England, and see that it is but a rude precursor of the product of the modern kiln. The hand-wrought nails are another reminder of the toilsomeness of early achievement; and lastly there is the beam, supposed to be another relic of the first house, the side of which is indented with holes for the reception of the wooden pegs which were used for joinings before nails of any sort were to be had.

Most of the attic accumulation has been taken away by the successive generations of those departing children of the old stock who wished to bear with them some reminder of the home place and of their birthright. Still the antique brass lantern yonder in the corner, its peaked top and the round holes in its metal sides which served to emit the light of the candle within, is not without interest; nor yet the old mirror frames, hair trunks, the "Yankee baker" by the chimney, the huge scoop and sugar scales that belonged to Major Alden of

Revolutionary days, and the ledger begun in 1771. Modern as these things are in the history of the house, they seem old to us unattached Americans of the Twentieth century.

Descending, we pass once more into the open air, but before leaving let us take a peep into the cellar. It is entered from an out-door cellarway on the eastern side of the house. The floor of it is roughly cobbled with untrimmed stones, and the walls are built up in a similar manner. We find large chunks of mortar fallen from the poorly joined masonry, and it seems a wonder that workmanship so crude should have endured so well. Overhead are the great under beams of the house. We need not be very tall to reach up to them, and one we find is partially decayed — another relic of the first dwelling, the house historian tells you.

Once more in the open air. The sun is shining — an hour higher in the sky — with same white brilliance with which he shone one, two, three hundred years ago,— when the house was building, before the house was. Indeed, it is the same white brilliance with which he shone a thousand years, or ten or a hundred thousand years ago: how long, who can say? The house seems old to us, but it is old only in comparison with the human life of its builders. Compared with the sun's life it has stood but an hour. Even the plains and the hills, and over yonder, just concealed from us, the ocean,—the hoary and venerable features of the earth,—are in infancy beside the sun's years.

It seems odd that living, creative intelligence should be the most fleeting and evanescent of all things in the panorama of Nature, so that a bare tenement of wood, built for a day, outlasts its builder, and the generations of his descendants. Yet we know that to him this house seemed but a day's resting place in the course of the soul's life, and surely the children of those who surrendered so much for the integrity of their faith may cling fast to this noblest article of their credo — that after the earth had claimed its own, the soul shall live again, the better life of its earthly building.

Again the steam whistle and again we are roused from revery. So we bid farewell to ths final earthly abiding place of those who came as Pilgrims seeking freedom for conscience sake. Plain and unpretentious we have found it, yet is it eloquent in every board and beam of the higher life and higher ideals in whose cause it was reared. And when, departing, we learn that the present master of the house is a John Alden and that the daughter of the house is a Priscilla, we cannot but feel that there is good and appropriate augury in this for the future of a family which so carefully honors its names and traditions. May they ever continue the good and substantial part which those of the blood of Alden have played in their country's upbuilding.

CHAPTER XII.

ALDENS of LATER DAYS.

COMPLETE genealogy of the descendants of John Alden and Priscilla, supposing that such a work were possible, would comprise many thousand names. Reckoning an average increase of three for each person born into the family, there would be in the eighth and ninth generations alone nearly ten thousand names, while the tenth generation, already in early youth, would add almost twice as many again. This rate is high for the present increase, since families such as adorned our fathers' households are not often to be met with nowadays, but for former times an average increase of three is much too modest a figure. In the first five generations of the family, for example, it was exceeded in the name of Alden alone, without taking into account the progeny of the daughters who married into other families. It is safe to say that the rate named has been maintained at least through the eighth generation, and that no Pilgrim blood has percolated further through American society than that of Alden.

Miss Abigail Thayer. Rev. Marcus Alden Tolman.
Rev. Edmund Kimball Alden. Miles Standish Alden.

But perhaps even more than by its healthy increase, the wonderful vitality of the race is evidenced by the longevity of its members, characteristic from the first generation down. The Pilgrim founder of the family died in his eighty-seventh year, but many of his descendants have exceeded him in age. Three, at least, have scored the full century — John Alden of Middleborough, Mass., born 1718, died 1821; Abigail Alden, who married Zephaniah Leonard, born 1744, died 1845; and Mrs. David Burnett of Cape Vincent on the St. Lawrence, who celebrated her one hundred second birthday in 1901. Elizabeth Pabodie was the first of the family to pass the age of ninety, but there have been many after her.

Eighty years is no uncommon age among Alden descendants, while a glance at Ebenezer Alden's Genealogy conveys the impression that the more part of those who have lived to adult years have attained the three score and ten of Biblical promise. There are even now a number of instances of the co-existence of represntatives of four generations in the same family succession,— among the great-grandmothers may be mentioned Mrs. Catherine Alden Alden of Janesville, Wis., and Mrs. Ella Alden Sullivan of Brockton, Mass., while Mrs.

David Burnett, above referred to, is credited with having gathered about her representatives of five generations of her own descendants — a record that outdoes even Elizabeth Pabodie's, who was a grandmother's grandmother in her own lifetime.

Mr. Henry Sherman Alden of Chautauqua county, New York, is one of the oldest male descendants of the Pilgrim, having been born in 1821. He has in his possession an interesting heirloom from his forefather, a picture of which may be seen on another page. It is an old snow-shoe concerning which he writes: "It is so moth-eaten that there is no beauty in it; it came down through the generations as one that John got from the tribe of Indians near Plymouth; it has no nails or wire, but is made of buckskin and seaweed, well braided." Miss Abigail Thayer of Boston was born in 1805, daughter of Deacon Eliphaz Thayer of Braintree. Her father was a Revolutionary soldier, and in recognition of his services Miss Thayer was presented with a gold spoon by the Society of the Daughters of the American Revolution. Miss Thayer is the survivor of a family of fourteen children,—a typical old-time Alden family. It is recorded of another Alden-connected Thayer, Ephraim, who married a daughter of the Pilgrims' daughter, that he, his wife and fourteen married children on one occasion went together to communion.

That the proverbial size of the Alden family is not wholly of the past is evidenced by the family of Mr. Charles L. Alden of Hyde Park. The group is shown on another page, and, as evidence of the strength of family tradition, includes the names John and Priscilla, Ruth and Miles Standish. The family mourns the recent loss of a baby son and brother, Bradford. It may be of interest to note that among the Alden descendants not all are of the goodly stature accredited to the first John. Probably the famous Tom Thumb, made famous by Barnum, was the most diminutive of the Aldens.

The life activities of men of the Alden descent have been manifold in kind and prolific in achievement. The record of fifty years of magisterial service to Plymouth Colony by the first John Alden has been an inspiring example to his successors in the name and the blood. They have never been men to shirk public service, and they have always taken a keen and active interest in civic affairs. A glance at the titles of some of the pamphlets and printed pleas issued over Alden names is a fair index of the aggressive type of citizenship which they stand for: "Despotism vs. Republicanism,"

Chapters from "Vaticanism Unmasked, by a Puritan of the Nineteenth Century," "Emancipation and Emigration"—a plan for the settlement of Southern freedmen in the West; and more recently a declaration that the Boer Republics "are and of right ought to be free."

In this connection we must not forget Noah Alden and his contentions for religious freedom in the Massachusetts of earlier days, nor yet the services of the two Presidents Adams, descended from John Alden through Ruth, the wife of John Bass, — of the first for our national liberty, of the second for the abolition of slavery. The family of Bradford is another prominent in Massachusetts political life into which has entered a strong infusion of Alden blood. The sinews of American statehood have been not a little strengthened by such infusions.

But it is not alone for civic services that the name of Alden has been prominent. From the first the race has had a strong leaning toward military duties. Doubtless all the sons of John the Pilgrim were members of the local militia. Two, at least, John, Jr., and Jonathan, attained prominence in military life. The descendants of the latter, especially, have always shown themselves ready to respond to the nation's call, and there has been hardly a generation in which the old house at Duxbury has not sent forth father or son to fight the country's battles. In the war of the Revolution the sons of Col. Briggs Alden, then the head of the household at Duxbury and himself a prominent advocate of Colonial rights, were among the first to volunteer. One son, Samuel, was mortally wounded in an expedition to the Penobscot River against the British in 1778. A second son, Judah, who afterward succeeded to the old homestead, served throughout the war as a trusted and skillful officer, attaining the rank of major.

Col. Ichabod Alden, a descendant of David, the Pilgrim's youngest son, was another valiant officer in the Revolution who lost his life in the service of the country. He was killed by Indian mercenaries of the British in northern New York in November, 1778. Maj. Roger Alden was an aide of General Greene in the War of Independence, and his son Bradford, who was with General Scott on the frontier, was an instructor at West Point and at one time commàndant there. Many others of the name and many of the descent served in the Revolutionary War, and the like may be said of all the wars that have followed.

Among the Aldens serving in the Civil War we are not surprised to find the present head of the family at Duxbury, preserving the military tradition of his line. Gen. Alonzo Alden of Troy, N. Y., won distinction in the same great conflict. The navy, too, has received eminent service from the family. In the early days many Aldens beside Captain John of Boston were sea captains, so that the family afforded good material for this service. The most eminent was Rear Admiral James Alden, who died in 1877. He served both in the Mexican and Civil Wars, and in the latter conflict was in command of the Richmond at New Orleans and of the Brooklyn at Mobile Bay and Fort Fisher. Rev. Charles Henry Alden, an accomplished scholar and teacher, served for several years as chaplain in the United States Navy, dying at Pensacola, Florida, in 1846, in consequence of severe hospital labors brought on by the Mexican War,— a noble representative of the Church Militant.

In all the higher professions the family has been well represented throughout our colonial and national history. In looking through the records of these professions, however, one is likely to be surprised to find that the law has apparently proven the least attractive to the descendants of the Plymouth magistrate. Still there are several who have attained eminence in this field. Perhaps the earliest to take up the ancestral employment was Squire Daniel Alden (1691-1767) of Stafford, Conn., who combined the duties of magistrate and farmer. Cyrus Alden, Esq., (1785-1855) was a practising lawyer in Boston in the early years of the century and the author of a legal text-book. He also possessed a lively interest in family history and made one of the earliest efforts to secure a general reunion of Pilgrim John Alden's descendants. Charles Alden of Ludlow, Mass., (1803-1862) served eighteen years as justice of the peace. General Alonzo Alden was a practising attorney in the state of New York, and Judge Geo. C. Alden, who died in Colorado in 1888, was another civil war veteran eminent in this profession.

But the law cannot fairly be named a competitor with medicine, which for many years has drawn a goodly number of Alden descendants. Dr. Abiathar Alden of Scarborough, Me., a physician and, it is said, also a metaphysician, enjoys the rather unenviable distinction of having been perhaps the only Alden who was a Tory at the time of the Revolutionary War. Dr. Seth Alden (1749-1809) of Caldwell, N. Y., attended in the family of Ethan Allen.

Dr. Howard Alden practised in Suffield, Conn., where in 1790 he built the residence now known as "Aldenheim" and still occupied by his descendants.

Dr. Enoch Alden of the same generation (the sixth from John of Mayflower fame) was a surgeon of uncommon ability, and became famous by reason of the successful substitution of an animal bone for a diseased human bone. Dr. Ebenezer Alden, Sr., also of this generation, was a practitioner and medical instructor of prominence at Randolph, Mass. His brother, Dr. Isaac Alden of Plainfield, N. H., was one of his pupils. His son, Dr. Ebenezer Alden, Jr., added to his professional abilities scholarly tastes and that lively interest in genealogy which prompted the publication of his work on the Alden family in 1867 — a work whose value is ever more and more appreciated by his successors in the field. He was also a writer on medical topics. Charles Henry Alden of Philadelphia, U. S. A. medical staff, was a contributor to the literature of army medicine and practise. These are but a few of the earlier representatives of the family in this calling.

Pedagogy is another profession which has called forth its full quota from the family, though in the earlier days it was rather a secondary than a pri-

A TYPICAL ALDEN FAMILY.

mary profession, the teacher usually being subordinate to the minister. The first ecclesiastical educator in the family, of eminent attainment in that work, was the Rev. Timothy Alden, D. D., (1771-1839). He was a graduate of Harvard College, where he attained high rank as a student of Oriental languages. During a life-time of unceasing and varied activity he founded no less than seven educational institutions, among them what is now Alleghany College, of which he was the first president. Rev. Joseph Alden, D. D., a friend of the poet Bryant, was professor of rhetoric in Williams College, of moral philosophy and metaphysics in Lafayette College, and finally was president of Jefferson College for a number of years. He was a prolific writer on many subjects, ranging from "Elements of Intellectual Philosophy" and "Science of Government" to works of fiction. Rev. John Alden (1806-1894) was at the head of Franklin Academy at Shelburne Falls, Mass., for a number of years.

The educational work of Dr. Ebenezer Alden, Sr., has already been referred to. Rev. Charles Henry Alden, whose connection with the navy has been mentioned, previous to that time taught and preached in Rhode Island, New Jersey, and finally in Philadelphia, where he opened a high school for young ladies. Abner Alden, graduated from Brown University in 1787, was a teacher and published several text-books in English branches early in the Nineteenth century. More recently Raymond McDonald Alden, of the University of Pennsylvania, has published in the same line "The Art of Debate" and a study of "The Rise of Formal Satire in England Under the Classical Influence." At the present day there are several other representatives of the family on the faculties of our colleges and universities.

But among all the professions, if one were to be chosen as most characteristic of the Aldens, that one could only be the ministry. The family's contribution to this profession has been continuous from the fourth generation, and affords, perhaps, the best examples of the varied and aggressive activities so natural to the race. If Jonathan Alden was pre-eminently the father of soldiers, his brother Joseph was no less characteristically an ancestor of ministers, the great majority of the clergymen of the family springing from his line. The first Alden divine, so far as is known to the writer, was Joseph's grandson, the Rev. Noah Alden (1725-1797) whose early stand for religious freedom has already been mentioned. He began his ministerial career as a Congregationalist, but later became a Baptist, thus serving the two churches which his kinsmen have always most favored. Rev. Timothy Alden of Yarmouth, Mass., (1736-1828), another descendant of Joseph, served nearly sixty years as pastor of one people. The educational work of his son, Rev. Timothy Alden, D.D., has already been mentioned, but it must not be forgotten that in connection with this work he continuously preached and even found time for missionary tours among the Indians of western New York and Pennsylvania.

Rev. Abishai Alden (1765-1833) was a Congregationalist minister in Connecticut. Rev. Seth Alden (1790-1813) died in a pulpit which he was supplying at Westborough, Mass. Rev. John Alden of Ashfield, Mass., (1761-1842) was a Baptist minister and farmer who gained a reputation for eccentricity because of his unconventional way of proclaiming the word of the Lord. His son, Rev. John Alden of Providence, R. I., was a teacher, as noted above, for many years active in the ministry, and finally ten years agent for southern New England of the American and Foreign Bible Society. Two sons of Dr. Ebenezer Alden, Jr., Ebenezer and

Edmund Kimball, held pastorates in the Congregational Church at Marshfield, Mass., and South Boston, respectively. At the former place Rev. Ebenezer preached the funeral sermon of Daniel Webster.

Rev. Charles Henry Alden and Rev. Joseph Alden, D.D., who have already been mentioned, were brothers, and descended from Joseph Alden of the second generation, as were all the other clergymen mentioned. Rev. Lucius Alden (1796-1884), a graduate of Brown and Andover, was in earlier years a missionary in the American West, and later pastor of prominent New England churches. He was born in East Bridgewater, Mass., and remembered the place of his nativity by a bequest of one hundred acres of valuable land, and the church society of his youth by a legacy of forty acres and his library. Rev. Marcus Alden Tolman, of Bethlehem, Pa., an Episcopal rector of scholarly and antiquarian tastes, is of this same ancestry. Many of the daughters of the family have married ministers.

It is related of the Rev. Francis Winter, who married Abigail Alden, grand-daughter of David, that he brought into Maine the first carriage ever seen in that state. It was a two-wheeled chaise which he procured for his wife on a long journey from Maine to Connecticut. Traveling was so difficult that two negroes were employed to accompany them with shovels and axes to clear the road. But upon his return, the minister's parishioners objected to such worldly vanity on their pastor's part, and he was compelled to dispose of his vehicle. That was in 1771. Diaries or journals of those pastors of early days would afford interesting reading to their posterity.

If Longfellow exaggerated the Pilgrim John's literary bent, as some suppose, it cannot be denied that a predilection for literature has yet been markedly characteristic of later members of the family, indicating some hereditary trend in that direction. The Aldens have always been prolific writers. We have already alluded to various types of professional writings — military, medical, legal, pedagogic, and the religious literature of many published sermons and addresses. These were the natural outcome of the professions which their authors followed.

But there is also a considerable body of what is called pure literature by Alden descendants. The names of the poets, Longfellow and Bryant, who trace their descent to John Alden through Elizabeth Pabodie and Anna Alden Snell, daughter of Zachariah Alden, respectively, are by far the most famous. Longfellow may fairly be named, too, the laureate of the family. Dr. Joseph Alden, a friend of Bryant's, and editor of his works, published over seventy volumes of one sort and another, among them several works of fiction. William Livingstone Alden, his son, a New York journalist, has published several works, for the most part humorous. Mrs. Isabella Alden, "Pansy," has written many religious sketches for the young. Mrs. Daniel Lothrop, "Margaret Sidney," is likewise a writer for the young. Mrs. Marian Longfellow O'Donoghue, niece of the poet, is a prominent Washington journalist, and writes, mainly in patriotic vein, both prose and graceful verse. Cynthia Alden Westover is the author of "Manhattan, Historic and Artistic." Mrs. Jane G. Austin has written a number of entertaining historical novels, dealing with early Plymouth, among them "Standish of Standish" and "Betty Alden." Her brother, John O. Goodwin, is the author of the most authentic history yet written of Plymouth, "The Pilgrim Republic." Alden Bradford has also written on historical topics. Ezra Judson Alden has written much on religious subjects. The historical works of the Hon. Charles Francis Adams, continuing his family's interest in the life of the nation, have given him a wide and enduring reputation.

In speculative lines we have the works of Henry Mills Alden, "God in His World; An Interpretation," and "A Study of Death;" also, "A Theory of the Structure of Matter," published by James S. Alden in 1896. Nor must we forget the work of Joseph Alden, above mentioned, in this field. But any mention of the literary labors and interests of the Alden descent would be most inadequate if it were to omit those genealogical and antiquarian productions, the outcome of an honest reverence for their Pilgrim source, which have served to maintain a family unity and enthusiasm rare indeed in this nation of scattering kindreds. Foremost among these is, of course, Timothy Alden's unique "Collection of American Epitaphs and Inscriptions," a rare work often heretofore alluded to in these pages, and Dr. Ebenezer Alden's "Memorial." Another work which has atttracted widespread interest is Rev. John Alden's "Autobiography," written in his eighty-third year, which contains much bearing on the family history.

More recently Mrs. Charles L. Alden of Troy,

N. Y., has contributed several chapters of an Alden "Genealogy" to the New England Historical and Genealogical Register, a work whose importance can be only measured by its magnitude. Finally, before dismissing, in this partial reference, the Alden contribution to our national literature, we should not fail to recall the noteworthy work of the publisher, John B. Alden, who was pioneer in the cheap production of English classics, a movement which has long since rendered the best literature in the language available to all.

To catalogue ever so briefly the business callings and successes of the Alden descent were a task impossible. They have made their way into every field of productive activity and everywhere the count of those who have achieved has far exceeded count of the failures.

They have brought to their work Yankee ingenuity and Yankee integrity — two traits that are not small factors in our nation's greatness, — and whether that work has been on the farm or in the shop or yet in the centres of exchange, they have given it a quality and high standard which have brought respect to the name and reflected honor upon the lineage. Enterprise, invention, versatility, — these are, perhaps, the best terms in which

THE MODERN PRISCILLA.

to describe the genius peculiar to the family, characteristic of all its works. It is needless to add that these are also the terms which best describe the genius of the American people as a whole, that the Aldens, therefore, are, before all things else, most typically Americans. Surely no better eulogy could be pronounced upon them.

But before we close we must say a word for the daughters of Priscilla. The part they play in the upbuilding, even though it is mainly a silent part, little known to the world, is no less important and lasting than the achievements of their brothers and sons. Without their gentler guidance and, we may believe, wise insight and courage, such as made their ancestress famous, there would be far less in the family history to which the children of today look back with pride.

Here we cannot even give their number or their names — good, old-fashioned names with a plentiful sprinkling of Priscilla's, — much less any account of their doings. But a nephew of one of them, the late Mr. Gilbert Alden Tolman of Randolph, Mass., has published a brief account of her home domain — as it was in the early years of the century that is recently passed — and surely in closing this volume of Alden memories and traditions, we cannot do better than here transcribe some portion of his account of a typical home and typical matron of the family of a generation now gone by.

The house where Sarah Alden Tolman — Mr. Tolman's "Aunt Sally" — lived in those years still stands in the town of Holbrook, Mass., (formerly a part of Randolph).

Mr. Tolman writes reminiscently: "Of its many pleasant rooms the kitchen attracted us most, because the aroma from Aunt Sally's cooking dainties appealed more strongly to our youthful sensibilities. . . . This kitchen was just twenty feet square and proportionately high; to us, then, it seemed a mile. The knots in the unpainted floor slightly projected; the solid oak outside door opening directly into the kitchen was exactly seven feet high by three and one-half feet wide (some of the folks were tall and some broad), and the latch-string was always out; the fireplace was five feet long, four feet high and almost two feet deep, and the crane was just four feet long, with hooks and tramels to fit every pot and kettle; the mantel was six feet long by four inches wide, and held the tinder box, flint and steel — lucifer matches were not invented yet, — and two brass candle-sticks.

Higher up still hung crook-necked squashes marked, 'save the seeds', and ears of corn for next year's planting.

"The huge brick oven seemed equal to the State House dome, and when on fire quite as brilliant. The bread peel, with a hole cut in the handle, hung on a nail in the chimney corner. In the other corner was the old Farmer's Almanac which Aunt Sally consulted to regulate the sun, moon, and stars, and forecast the weather, and a file of which she preserved, reaching far back into the early years of the century. . . . The exact size of the oven I have lost, but I can give an approximate idea. The day before each Thanksgiving it baked at once fifty mince pies, with a huge plum pudding in the middle (not of the pies but of the oven), and then Aunt Sally reached the long-handled peel beyond the sight of mortal, and last, though not least, brought forth a generous pot of pork and beans, the crisp pork, cut and checked and scored, bursting through the confines of the succulent bean, all baked and all browned, just 'fit for a king.' . . . There was also room in the oven for the turkey; but, no, Aunt Sally didn't bake her turkeys. A tin kitchen was set before the open fire, the turkey impaled on a spindle was placed therein, and the cat and dog took turns at turning the spit (the spit was a spindle which was turned by a projecting crank). . . . The hearth was laid in four granite slabs, each about three feet square, and on them we cracked both fingers and shag-barks. The two fire-dogs were pig iron, — money would not buy them today. Cooking stoves had not arrived, and stones from the wall and coal from the mine were considered equally useless for cooking or heating purposes; four foot logs were used instead. . . .

"But the kitchen is incomplete without at least a limited description of Aunt Sally herself, the presiding genius there. Aunt Sally was a sweet singer, and, though a devout woman, we really think put singing paramount to praying. It was an Alden inheritance, her noted ancestor, John, who with Governor Bradford landed from the Mayflower on Plymouth Rock in 1620, for years lead the Congregational singing there, and Aunt Sally long sang in a neighboring church choir many years after. . . . Aunt Sally was proud, very proud, as all the Aldens were and are, but she had no enemies. She would sit and sing and spin all day long, but I never saw the old spinning wheel in the kitchen, as 'the fuzz would get into the food.' She kept sheep, she spun yarn, she knitted the family stockings, and through it all she sang. We don't say that her music was always harmonious, but the songs to us were always sweet."

Surely it is like Aunt Sally, tender, watchful, industrious, warding her household with motherly care and dignity, the song on her lips unstilled, and none the less sweet for the passing of time, that we must picture Priscilla, also, in her later, matronly years. And surely the picture is no less fair nor any less an inspiration to her daughters' daughters than that other earlier scene in which the poet has portrayed her singing as she spun. Let us therefore close our tale of memories with this image of sweet domesticity—symbolic of the force that has wrought whatever is best in the kindred of Alden.

Since the pen was laid aside from the foregoing writings, an event of warm interest to all of Alden descent has taken place. On August twenty-eight, 1902, several hundred of the kindred descendants met at the historic Duxbury homestead, and with ceremony and fellowship, organized a permanent society of "The Alden Kindred of America."

The year before, upon the initiative of Miss A. Ella Alden, a picnic meeting of Alden descendants was held at Avon, Mass., and it was attended with such spirit and enthusiasm that then and there arrangements were made for the greater coming together at Duxbury. Mr. A. E. Alden presiding, Mr. George W. Alden of Brockton, Mass., was made president, and with the aid of Messrs. Lewis Alden, of Holbrook, John W. Alden, of Duxbury, Charles L. Alden, of Hyde Park and other prominently interested, the historic gathering was prepared for. Meantime, it is interesting to note an "Alden Descendants' Society" was organized at Binghampton, New York, without knowledge of the New England movement, showing that the family spirit was widely aroused and the time ripe for a lasting organization.

The assigned day was one of unusual beauty, with blue, sunny sky, and an atmosphere lambently premonitious of Indian summer. A large tent near the old house was the place of gathering, and here the ceremonies of the day were held. President George W. Alden, occupying a chair once the property of Elder Brewster, called the meeting to order. Short addresses and singing were followed by the adoption of constitution

THE ALDEN KINDRED OF AMERICA, 1902.

and by-laws drawn up by Mr. Augustus E. Alden of Boston, who also christened the new society. Officers were elected for the year, and Rev. Marcus Alden Tolman, orator of the day, gratified the ears of the gathered kindred with an address, whose eloquent earnestness was dashed with more than one touch of the sly wit and graceful humor befitting a son of Priscilla. Perhaps with the fine figure which formed the orator's peroration, we may best engross the memory of this most significant day, for in it he draws the larger meaning which should underlie the pride of all who trace their descent, as we fondly say, from Plymouth Rock.

"One bright day in the month of August I stood upon the western shore of Lake Geneva, Switzerland, and tried to trace the outline of an Alpine range, sixty-five miles distant. The highest peak towered fifteen thousand feet above its base, yet, as it was covered with ice and snow, under the glare of the mid-day sun, it could not be distinguished from the clouds by which it was capped. But, as the day drew to a close, and the sun sank farther and farther in the West, the outline of the distant range appeared with greater and greater distinctness, until at last the rugged rocks and crags were lost in the twilight, while the snowy crests of the mountains threw back the sun's parting rays and stood forth in all their majestic grandeur, like piles of burnished silver. It was a sight never to be forgotten.

"So, like the distant Alpine range, stand the Pilgrims of 1620. Time has softened their asperities. Their rugged features are lost in the distance. By the alchemy of the ages the rock has turned to silver. We view them through the atmosphere of their influence upon America and American institutions. From their towering moral heights, 'pure as ice, chaste as snow,' there is thrown back a reflection of that Sun which guided the Pilgrims' wandering feet to these western shores; that Sun in whose light those Pilgrims ever basked; that Sun which never goes down, but whose rays shine brighter and brighter 'unto the perfect day.'"

CHAPTER XIII.

THE ALDEN AND MOLINES ARMS.

THE use of armorial bearings to distinguish family and rank arose some time during the Twelfth century. Previous to that time it had been customary for knights to adorn their shields with symbols and designs commemorating their military achievements, much in the mode and spirit of the American Indian who paints his deeds upon his ceremonial shirt of deer-skin. But with the development of defensive armor, and especially with the adoption of the closed helmet, which concealed the face of the wearer, it became necessary that war-leaders should assume some badge or token by means of which their followers could distinguish them in the press of battle.

Thus it came about that fixed and individual arms were widely used for this purpose, blazoned on shield or broidered on surcoat, and thence, eventually, stamped upon all the properties of their knightly bearer. They became hereditary, too, and even transferable like other property, so that in time many men might bear the same coat. From this arose confusion, for the straightening of which the College of Heraldry was evolved.

The sovereign assumed the sole right of granting the use of armorial bearings, which in each case were prepared by the official Heralds according to a strict etiquette as to the rank of the bearer and the design to which his rank entitled him. The granting of a coat of arms was then esteemed a patent of "nobility," and is so still on the continent, though in England the term "noble" has come to be restricted to members of the peerage.

In Europe the title to armorial bearings is governed by two main tenets of Heraldric law: (1) The holder must be a member of the family to whom the coat was granted, and no two families may hold the same coat; and (2) he must be a lineal descendant of the person to whom the coat was given. Furthermore the cadets of any house are only entitled to the parent arms with some modification indicative of their cadency, and the daughters have no title to arms except they be heiresses. Neither can a mother transmit to her children a right to bearings which are hers except as quartered on the father's shield.

In America only the national and state arms have official sanction or obtain legal recognition.

The use of family crests and coats is an arbitrary assumption on the part of individuals which only in the rarest cases — one in a thousand — would be recognized as legitimate by European Heralds. At the same time the usage as established in this country is not only legitimate but praiseworthy; for it aims at nothing more than family demarcation and the sustaining of ancient traditions.

Where descent can be traced with probability (few, indeed, are the certain genealogies) to some mediaeval family of note the best possible means of distinguishing Americans sprung from a common stock is their common adoption of the characteristic arms of that family. Surnames are no longer adequate marks of family distinction. Not only is the same name frequently borne by families totally unrelated, yet of common nationality, but the cosmopolitan influx of Europeans into the United States has given rise to a vast number of families who bear old English surnames, either arbitrarily assumed or formed by the Anglicization of foreign names. It is well, therefore, for those who wish to preserve family or national tradition to assume some sign which will indicate the stock from whence they are sprung.

In selecting a coat of arms for this purpose,

either some definite coat granted to a known forebear may be taken, or a coat may be made up from the essential characteristics common to the various coats found in the family. The latter method is likely to produce the more artistic result and serves the purpose equally well. But it should always be borne in mind that from the European point of view the American usage is pure assumption.

The armorial bearings which the descendants of the Pilgrim John Alden have most widely used are the arms of the Aldens of Hertford and Middlesex, whence it seems most probable that he sprung. The oldest coat in this family of which we have record was granted to John Alden of the Middle Temple in 1607. This coat is described with slight differences in the various encyclopedias of heraldry. The oldest description that we have is in Guillim's "Display of Heraldry," published in 1610. It runs as follows:

"He beareth Gules, three Crescents within a Bordure engrail'd Ermine by the name of Alden. This Coat was assign'd (September 8, 1607.) by William Cambden, Clarencieux, to John Alden of the Middle Temple."

Guillim does not describe the crest accompanying this shield, but it is given in Berry's "Encyclopaedia of Heraldry" together with a slightly altered description of the shield:

"Alden (Hertf. and of the Temple, London) gu. a bezant between three crescents, within a bordure, engr. erm. Crest: out of a ducal coronet per pale gu. and sa. a demi-lion or. (Granted 1607.)"

Berry also describes three other Alden coats, two of which manifestly belong in this same family (one is identical with Guillim's description). The third is described: "Or, a bat's wing gu. surmounted of another az. Crest: out of a coronet arg. two wings as in the coat." A third variation upon the crescent blazoned coat is given by Edmonson: "Gu. a mullet arg. between three crescents erm. within bordure engr. of the second." In "Fairbank's Crests" three are given for Aldens: "Out of a ducal coronet or, a demi-lion gu." "Out of a ducal coronet per pale gu. and sa., a demi-lion rampant or." "Out of a coronet arg., a bat's wing gu., surmounted of another arg."

Doubtless many of these variations are modified forms of the original, borne by cadets in the family, but even with identical coats the descriptions vary, and it will be seen how difficult it is to reconstruct the original with historical accuracy. The chief characteristics, however, both of crest and coat are easily recognizable.

In Burke's "General Armory" are given more than twenty-five coats of arms as pertaining to families of the name of Molyneux, Molineux, Molines, Molynes, Mullines, Mullins. All of these trace their descent to Norman and French families, and most of them to the Molyneux, or Molineaux, as it is sometimes better spelled, who left the fortress of Molineaux-sur-Seine to follow William the Conqueror to England.

The family was represented as early as 1423 by a Baron Molynes who bore arms described (Burke): "Paly wavy of six or and gu." In Rietstap's "Armorial General" is described the almost identical coat of the Norman family of Moulins: "Pale-onde d'or et de gueules," and it can hardly be that this dual similarity of name and bearings is mere coincidence. The most distinguished English branch are the Molineux of Lancaster from which are descended the Earls of Sefton. Guillim gives an interesting paragraph upon the arms of Richard de Molineux, temp. Richard II, which shows a truly scholastic appreciation of the possibilities of trifles. But in those days Heraldry was a fine art and a field of much astute learning:

"The Field is Azure, a Cross moline pierced Lozengways Or. This is the second Form of Piercing before-mentioned, and the Coat was born by Richard de Molineux of Lancaster, that lived in the Reign of King Richard the Second. Concerning this Cross moline (saith Leigh) that if it stood Saltire-ways, then should you call it Ferre de Molin, that is to say, a Mill rind, or the Ink of a Mill: Which to me, seemeth a very paradox and* Transposition (being a Thing merely accidental) should give a new Denomination to the Thing Transposed, and, consequently, alter the Essence thereof: Quia novum nomen dat novum esse rei; where are new Names, new Things are supposed to be. It were a Thing worthy of Admiration, that Accidents should have such Power in them: For Aristotle, Physicorum I. saith, Accidentia possunt Miraculose, & non alias mutare subjectum; Accidents change not their Subject but by Miracle. Addition, doubtless, and Subtraction, are of greater Force than Transmutation or Location; yet there is no such Power in them as that they can alter the Essence of any Thing: Quia augmentum vel diminutio (saith Chassanaeus) circa accidentia contractuum, non reponunt contractum in diverso esse,

*For "and" we should probably read "that."

neque per ea intelligitur ab eo in substantialibus recessus: The Adding or Diminishing of Accidents, makes not the Thing lose the Nature of his Being."

The crest to this coat of Richard de Molineux is given by Burke: "Out of a chapeau gules turned up ermine a peacock's tail proper," (i. e., natural colors). The same authority describes the arms of the Earls of Sefton, who are descended from this Richard, as follows: "Azure, a cross moline or. Crest: A chapeau gules turned up ermine adorned with a plume of peacock feathers proper. Supporters: Two lions azure. Motto: Vivere sat vincere." It will be seen that this is only an elaborated form of the earlier coat; and with modifications, but generally characterized by the cross moline upon an azure field, it is borne by many, of the names Molyneux and Molines.

The choice of a coat of arms for its historical interest and associations is well and good, but as a family badge — a badge which will distinguish a particular stock from others of the name, or discriminate various persons as of one ancestry — the right to the badge must be unique and unmistakeable. This cannot be claimed for the descendants of John Alden and Priscilla with respect to either

National Monument to the Forefathers, Plymouth.

the Alden or the Molineux arms, even in this country. There are other families of Alden now in the country and many of Molineux and Mullins.

What the American Aldens are chiefly anxious to preserve is the integrity of the family of the Pilgrim John. Holding in mind that the origin of armorial bearings was in the symbolic picturing of knightly achievements, the deeds which gave their doers fame, would it not be well for the children of the most famous of American lovers to adopt insignia commemorating the story? Such insignia would be uniquely theirs, and it would date to a year barely a dozen twelve months after the first Alden coat of arms of which we have record was granted, and a hundred years before the first Earl of Sefton. In the language of Heraldry such a coat might be described:

They bear them Azure, a spinning-wheel Or (the Molines' colors). And for crest, a great Pilgrim hat, Sable with a buckle Or, plain as is most appropriate for him who loved best to be known as "plain John Alden," and hovering shelteringly over the symbol of the gentle Priscilla. And for motto, they bear (here is no question): "Prithee, why don't you speak for yourself, John?"

APPENDIX.

JOHN ALDEN, Anagram, END AL ON HI.

(From Governor Bradford's Journal.)

The names of those which came over first, in ye year 1620, and were by the blessing of God the first beginers and (in a sort) the foundation of all the Plantations and Colonies in New-England; and their families.

Mr. John Carver; Katherine, his wife; Desire
8. Minter; & 2. man-servants, John Howland, Roger
Wilder; William Latham, a boy; & a maid servant, & a child yt was put to him, called Jasper More.

Mr. William Brewster; Mary, his wife; with 2. sons, whose names were Love & Wrasling; and a
6. boy was put to him called Richard More; and another of his brothers. The rest of his children were left behind, & came over afterwards.

Mr. Edward Winslow; Elizabeth, his wife; & 2.
5. men servants, caled Georg Sowle and Elias Story; also a litle girle was put to him, caled Ellen, the sister of Richard More.

William Bradford, and Dorothy, his wife; hav-
2. but one child, a sone, left behind, who came afterward.

Mr. Isaack Allerton, and Mary, his wife; with 3.
6. children, Bartholmew, Remember, & Mary; and a
servant boy, John Hooke.

Mr. Samuell Fuller, and a servant, caled Wil-
2. liam Butten. His wife was behind, & a child, which
came afterwards.

2. John Crakston, and his sone, John Crakston.

2. Captin Myles Standish, and Rose, his wife.

Mr. Christopher Martin, and his wife, and 2.
4. servants, Salamon Prower and John Langemore.

Mr. William Mullines, and his wife, and 2. chil-
5. dren, Joseph & Priscila; and a servant, Robert Carter.

Mr. William White, and Susana, his wife, and
6. one sone, caled Resolved, and one borne a ship-bord,
caled Peregriene; & 2. servants, named William
Holbeck & Edward Thomson.

Mr. Steven Hopkins, & Elizabeth, his wife, and
2. children, caled Giles, and Constanta, doughter,
8. both by a former wife; and 2. more by this wife,
caled Damaris & Oceanus; the last was borne at sea;
and 2. servants, called Edward Doty and Edward
Litster.

Mr. Richard Warren; but his wife and children
1. were lefte behind, and came afterwards.

John Billinton, and Elen, his wife; and 2. sones.
4. John & Francis.

Edward Tillie, and Ann, his wife; and 2. chil-
4. dren that were their cossens, Henery Samson and
Humillity Coper.

John Tillie, and his wife; and Eelizabeth, their
3. doughter.

Francis Cooke, and his sone John. But his wife
2. & other children came afterwards.

Thomas Rogers, and Joseph, his sone. His
2. other children came afterwards.

3. Thomas Tinker, and his wife, and a sone.

2. John Rigdale, and Alice, his wife.

James Chilton, and his wife, and Mary, their
3. doghter. They had an other doughter, yt was
maried, came afterward.

Edward Fuller, and his wife, and Samuell, their
3. sonne.

John Turner, and 2. sones. He had a doughter
3. came some years after to Salem, wher she is now
living.

Francis Eaton, and Sarah, his wife, and Sam-
3. uell, their sone, a yong child.

Moyses Fletcher, John Goodman, Thomas Wil-
10. liams, Digerie Preist, Edmond Margeson, Peter

Browne, Richard Britterige, Richard Clarke, Richard Gardenar, Gilbart Winslow.

John Alden was hired for a cooper, at South-
1. Hampton, wher the ship victuled; and being a hopfull yong man, was much desired, but left to his
owne liking to go or stay when he came here; but
he stayed, and maryed here.

John Allerton and Thomas Enlish were both
hired, the later to goe mr. of a shalop here, and ye
2. other was reputed as one of ye company, but was to
go back (being a seaman) for the help of others behind. But they both dyed here, before the shipe
returned.

There were allso other 2. seamen hired to stay a
2. year here in the country, William Trevore, and one
Ely. But when their time was out, they both returned.

These, bening aboute a hundred sowls, came over in this first ship; and began this worke, which God of his goodnes hath hithertoo blesed; let his holy name have ye praise.

And seeing it hath pleased him to give me to see 30. years compleated since these beginings; and that the great works of his providence are to be observed, I have thought it not unworthy my paines to take a veiw of the decreasings & increasings of these persons, and such changs as hath pased over them & theirs, in this thirty years. It may be of some use to such as come after; but, however, I shall rest in my owne benefite.

I will therfore take them in order as they lye.

Mr. Carver and his wife dyed the first year; he in ye spring, she in ye somer; also, his man Roger and ye litle boy Jasper dyed before either of them, of ye commone infection. Desire Minter returned to her freinds, & proved not very well, and dyed in England. His servant boy Latham, after more than 20. years stay in the country, went into England, and from thence to the Bahamy Ilands in ye West Indies, and ther, with some others, was starved for want of food. His maid servant maried, & dyed a year or tow after, here in this place.

His servant, John Howland, maried the doughter of John Tillie, Elizabeth, and they are both now
15. living; and have 10. children, now all living; and their eldest daughter hath 4. children. And ther 2. daughter, 1. all living; and other of their children mariagable. So 15. are come of them.

Mr. Brewster lived to a very old age; about 80. years he was when he dyed, having lived some 23. or 24. years here in ye countrie; & though his wife

dyed long before, yet she dyed aged. His sone
4. Wrastle dyed a yonge man unmaried; his sone Love
lived till this year 1650, and dyed, & left 4. children,
now living. His doughters which came over after
him are dead, but have left sundry children alive;
his eldest sone is still liveing, and hath 9. or 10.
2. children; one maried, who hath a child or 2.

Richard More his brother dyed the first winter;
4. but he is maried, and hath 4. or 5. children, all
living.

Mr. Ed: Winslow his wife dyed the first winter;
2. and he maried with the widow of Mr. White, and
hath 2. children living by her mariagable, besids
sundry that are dead.

One of his servants dyed, as also the litle girle,
8. soone after the ships arivall. But his man, Georg
Sowle, is still living, and hath 8. childre.

William Bradford his wife dyed soone after their
4. arivall; and he maried againe; and hath 4. children,
3. wherof are maried.

Mr. Allerton his wife dyed with the first, and
his servant, John Hooke. His sone Bartle is maried in England, but I know not how many children
he hath. His doughter Remember is maried at
Salem, & hath 3. or 4. children living. And his
8. doughter Mary is maried here, & hath 4. children.

Him selfe maried againe with ye doughter of Mr. Brewster, & hath one sone living by her, but she is long since dead. And he is maried againe, and hath left this place long agoe. So I account his increase to be 8. besids his sons in England.

Mr. Fuller his servant dyed at sea; and after his
2. wife came over, he had tow children by her, which are living and growne up to years; but he dyed some 15. years agoe.

John Crakston dyed in the first mortality; and about 5. or 6. years after, his sone dyed; having lost him selfe in ye wodes, his feet became frosen, which put him into a feavor, of which he dyed.

Captain Standish his wife dyed in the first sick-
4. nes, and he maried againe, and hath 4. sones liveing, and some are dead.

Mr. Martin, he & all his, dyed in the first infection not long after the arivall.

Mr. Molines, and his wife, his sone, and his servant, dyed the first winter. Only his dougter Pris-
15. cila survied, and maried with John Alden, who are both living, and have 11. children. And their eldest daughter is maried, & hath five children.

Mr. White and his 2. servants dyed soone after ther landing. His wife maried with Mr. Winslow
7. (as is before noted.) His 2. sons are maried, and

Resolved hath 5. children, Perigrine tow, all living.
So their increase are 7.

Mr. Hopkins and his wife are now both dead
but they lived above 20. years in this place, and had
one sone and 4. doughters borne here. Ther sone
5. became a seaman & dyed at Barbadoes; one daughter
dyed here and 2. are maried; one of them hath 2.
children; & one is yet to mary. So their increase
4. which still survive are 5. But his sone Giles
maried and hath 4. children.

His doughter Constanta is also maried, and hath
12. 12. children, all of them living, and one of them
maried.

Mr. Richard Warren lived some 4. or 5. years,
and had his wife come over to him, by whom he had
4. 2. sons before dyed; and one of them is maryed,
and hath 2. children. So his increase is 4. But he
had 5. doughters more came over with his wife, who
are all maried, & living, & have many children.

John Billinton, after he had bene here 10. yers,
8. was executed for killing a man; and his eldest sone
dyed before him; but his 2. sone is alive, and maried, & hath 8. children.

Edward Tillie and his wife both dyed soon after
7. their arivall; and the girle Humility, their cousen,
was sent for into England, and dyed ther. But the

youth Henery Samson is still liveing, and is maried, & hath 7. children.

John Tillie and his wife both dyed a litle after they came ashore; and their daughter Elizabeth maried with John Howland, and hath issue as is before noted.

Francis Cooke is still living, a very olde man,
and hath seene his children's children have chil-
8. dren; after his wife came over, (with other of his
children,) he hath 3. still living by her, all maried,
and have 5. children; so their encrease is 8. And
his sone John, which came over with him, is mar-
4. ied, and hath 4. children living.

Thomas Rogers dyed in the first sicknes, but his
6. sone Joseph is still living, and is maried, and hath
6. children. The rest of Thomas Rogers children came over, & are maried, & have many children.

Thomas Tinker and his wife and sone all dyed in the first sicknes.

And so did John Rigdale and his wife.

James Chilton and his wife also dyed in the first
10. infection. But their daughter Mary is still living,
and hath 9. children; and one daughter is maried, & hath a child; so their increase is 10.

Edward Fuller and his wife dyed soon after they

4. came ashore; but their sone Samuell is living &
maried, and hath 4. children or more.

John Turner and his 2. sones all dyed in the first siknes. But he hath a daughter still living at Salem, well maried, and approved of.

Francis Eaton his first wife dyed in the generall sicknes; and he maried againe, & his 2. wife dyed,
4. & he maried the 3. and had by her 3. children. One
of them is maried, & hath a child; the other are living, but one of them is an ideote. He dyed about 16. years agoe. His sone Samuell, who came over a
1. sucking child, is allso maried, & hath a child.

Moyses Fletcher, Thomas Williams, Digerie Preist, John Goodman, Edmond Margeson, Richard Britteridge, Richard Clarke. All these dyed sone after their arivall, in the generall sicknes that befell. But Digerie Preist had his wife & children sent hither afterwards, she being Mr. Allertons sister. But the rest left no posteritie here.

Richard Gardiner became a seaman, and died in England, or at sea.

Gilbert Winslow, after diverse years aboad here, returned into England, and dyed ther.

Peter Browne maried twise. By his first wife
6. he had 2. children, who are living, & both of them
maried, and the one of them hath 2. children; by

his second wife he had 2. more. He dyed about 16. years since.

Thomas English and John Allerton dyed in the generall siknes.

John Alden maried with Priscila, Mr. Mollines his doughter, and had issue by her as is before related.

Edward Doty & Edward Litster, the servants of Mr. Hopkins. Litster, after he was at liberty, went to Virginia, & ther dyed. But Edward Doty by a second wife hath 7. children, and both he and they are living.

Of these 100. persons which came over in this first ship together, the greater halfe dyed in the generall mortality; and most of them in 2. or three months time. And for those which survied, though some were ancient & past procreation, & others left ye place and cuntrie, yet of those few remaining are sprunge up above 160. persons, in this 30. years, and are now living in this presente year, 1650. besids many of their children which are dead, and come not within this account.

And of the old stock (of one & other) ther are yet living this present year, 1650. nere 30. persons. Let the Lord have ye praise, who is the High Preserver of men.